THE ULTIMATE GUIDE TO PAYING ZERO TAXES

RORY V. BROCK

Copyright © 2025 by Rory V. Brock. All rights reserved.

No part of this book, *The Ultimate Guide to Paying Zero Taxes*, may be reproduced, transmitted, or distributed in any form or by any means, including photocopying, recording, or any information storage and retrieval system, without prior written permission from the publisher, except as provided by applicable copyright law.

All trademarks, service marks, and trade names mentioned in this book are the property of their respective owners. The inclusion of any trade names or trademarks does not imply endorsement or affiliation with the author, publisher, or this book.

The Ultimate Guide to Paying Zero Taxes is a work of non-fiction intended for informational purposes only. The author and publisher make no representations or warranties about the completeness or accuracy of the information provided. This book is not intended to offer specific legal, financial, or tax advice. For advice on your specific circumstances, consult a qualified professional.

The publisher is not liable for any loss or damage, including but not limited to indirect or consequential damages, arising from the use of this book or its contents. The advice and strategies contained herein are based on the author's experience and research as of the publication date.

This book is dedicated to the working man—the average American who goes to work each day and pays his taxes. It is for those who have labored in factories and on assembly lines, building the very fabric of our country. To the HVAC workers, carpet cleaners, plumbers, electricians, and roofers, and to those who build chimneys and fireplaces. This book is for all who have mixed concrete under the hot sun or spent weeks drilling concrete in the dirt beneath houses. It is dedicated to the security guards, private investigators, and the kids who didn't like school and dropped out of college.

I can relate. I'm one of you.

—Rory

Author's Note: Finding My Purpose

To this day, it surprises me that I became an author of three books about money.

I didn't plan to write another book, but my friends thought I had found *the secret* to building wealth and paying no taxes, and they thought it was vitally important to share it.

I'll assume that you are not familiar with my story, and the story of how I became an author. But during the process, I found my purpose: to educate others about how money *really* works, and create lasting, transformative change that will ripple through generations.

This book is dual-purpose: It will teach you a simple but very effective tax strategy to help you achieve financial independence. And when you achieve financial independence, I hope you also find *your* purpose.

This book will be the foundation for every student and teacher in future classes of *The Perfect Portfolio*™ course—because I know its content is that powerful.

A Note to Financial Advisors

My goal is not to have all my readers fire their financial advisors. Remember, *I was one of you.*

I spent 15 years sitting across a kitchen table helping families implement strategies to save and invest.

I also believed I was doing the best for my clients . . . and I was . . . *with the knowledge and products that I had access to.*

If you are a financial advisor, I hope this book also helps you achieve financial freedom (at any age), and I hope you *use the knowledge you now have gained* to help others do the same.

CONTENT

Author's Note: Finding My Purpose.. 3
A Note to Financial Advisors.. 4
1.. 10
The Pandemic Epiphany.. 10
    How I Discovered The Perfect Portfolio™.. 10
2.. 14
Be S.M.A.R.T.... 14
    Strategies to Maximize Assets and Reduce Taxes................................. 14
3.. 19
What Is Money?.. 19
    Is a Cow Money?.. 19
4.. 23
The Millionaire Next Door.. 23
    Joe's Journey to $6 Million by Never Selling.. 23
5.. 28
Avoiding "Dead Money".. 28
    Invest in The Five Pillars That Can Secure Loans................................ 28
6.. 33
Financial Alchemy.. 33
    How to Transform "Bad Debt" into "Good Debt"................................ 33
PART ONE.. 38
Stocks and ETFs.. 38
    The First Pillar of a Buy, Borrow, Die Strategy...................................... 38
7.. 39
Buy Low and Never Sell.. 39
    Stocks and ETFs: The First Pillar of Buy, Borrow, Die........................ 40
8.. 43
Stocks and ETFs.. 43
    The Good, the Bad, and the Ugly.. 43
9.. 48
Buy More and Never Sell.. 48

    Using Fear and Greed to Amplify Your Returns.. 48

10...52
Buy, Borrow, Die..52
    It Really Is for Everyday Americans..52

11...56
The Basics of Financial Alchemy..56
    Press Buttons and Create Money!..56

12...60
IRA..60
    It IS a Retirement Account! (so Focus on Your Financial Independence)............... 60

13...63
Future-Proof Your Savings:..64
    Borrow to Fund the Tax Benefits of a Roth IRA... 64

14...68
Shielding Your Wealth..68
    Avoid Future Tax Hikes with a Backdoor Roth IRA.. 68

15...73
SPY vs SPY vs SPY..73
    One ETF, Three Outcomes.. 73

16...77
Municipal Bonds...77
    "Munis" for Tax-Free Money.. 77

17...81
Minimizing Your Tax Bill..81
    Strategies for Reducing Capital Gains Taxes... 81

18...85
Turning Losses into Gains..85
    How Tax-Loss Harvesting Can Save You Money... 85

19...88
Borrow, Again..89
    If You Can't Beat 'Em, Join 'Em... 89

PART TWO..93
Real Estate..93
    The second Pillar of a Buy, Borrow, Die strategy.. 93

20. 94
Unlocking Tax-Free Savings 94
The 2024 First-Time Homebuyers Tax Credit 94

21. 98
Leveraging OPM 98
The Tax-Efficient Path to Homeownership 98

22. 102
The Home Mortgage Deduction 102
Home Sweet Tax Break 102

23. 105
The $250,000/$500,000 Home Sale Exemption 106
Tax-Free Home Sale Jackpot 106

24. 109
Depreciation on Rental Property 110
Tax-Free Income for Real Estate Investors! 110

25. 113
Cost Segregation 114
Boosting Tax-Free Income for Real Estate Investors 114

26. 117
Bonus Depreciation 118
Supercharging Tax-Free Income for Real Estate Investors 118

27. 121
Business Ownership and Rental Income 122
Buy One to Live In and One to Rent 122

28. 125
Real Estate Professional Status 126
The "Secret Sauce" to Pay No Taxes 126

29. 130
The Home Office Deduction 131
Your Tax-Saving Super Weapon 131

30. 135
The Augusta Rule 136
Unlocking Tax-Free Income Through Short-Term Rentals 136

31. 139

The Short-Term Rentals Loophole..140
    A Powerful Tool for Tax Savings...140

32..144

House Hacking..145
    Transforming Your Home from Liability to Tax-Free Asset.....................145

PART THREE...150

Income and Asset Protection...150
    The third Pillar of a Buy, Borrow, Die strategy..150

33..150

Maximizing the Benefits of Term Life Insurance................................151
    Protecting Wealth with Smart Riders..151

34..154

Indexed Universal Life Insurance..155
    The Swiss Army Knife of Investing and Tax Avoidance..........................155

PART FOUR...159

Cryptocurrency..159
    The Fourth Pillar of a Buy, Borrow, Die strategy.....................................159

35..160

Bitcoin vs Bucks..160
    Why Digital Coins Beat the Unlimited Dollar Machine..........................160

36..163

Bitcoin ETFs...164
    The Smart Way to Hold Digital Gold Without the Hassle......................164

PART FIVE..168

Precious Metals..168
    The Fifth Pillar of a Buy, Borrow, Die strategy..168

37..169

Golden Opportunities..169
    Leveraging Buy, Borrow, Die to Acquire Gold and Precious Metals......169

PART SIX..174

Business Ownership..174
    The solid Foundation of a Buy, Borrow, Die strategy.............................174

38..174

Tacos, Tequila, and Tax Breaks..175

Maximizing Your Business Deductions...175

39. 180
S-Corp Secrets..180
How to Slash Your Taxes and Keep More of Your Money.................................180

40. 183
Turning Learning into Earning..184
Making Education a Business Expense.. 184

41. 187
Section 179 Savings...188
Buy a Tesla for Your Business... 188

42. 191
Tax-Savvy Health..192
How to Save on Taxes While Protecting Your Well-Being.................................192

43. 196
Year-End Tax Planning..197
Bigger Savings in the Final Stretch...197

PART SEVEN..202
Advanced Concepts..202
Improving the Performance of a Buy, Borrow, Die strategy............................202

44. 202
Rollover Danger...203
Why Great Returns May Not Be Great for You.. 203

45. 206
Finding a Fiduciary...207
Who Wants to Play Where's Waldo?.. 207

46. 210
Leveraging Correlation..211
Amplify Returns with the Buy, Borrow, Die Strategy..211

47. 214
Live off the Borrow Button..215
Unlocking Tax-Free Financial Freedom.. 215

48. 219
Will You Own Nothing and Be Happy?..220
Epilogue..225

Real Estate Simplified..228
How to Get Wealthy... Simplified..232
Glossary of Terms...236
Bonus Stock Report.. 242
Knowledge Quiz & Study Guide...246
    Part 1: Multiple-Choice Questions... 246
    Part 2: True or False.. 247
    Part 3: Short Answer Questions... 247
    Part 4: Case Studies & Application Scenarios...................................248
        Scenario 1: The Borrowing Dilemma... 248
        Scenario 2: The Real Estate Investor... 248
        Scenario 3: The Retirement Planner..248
    Part 5: Action Plan—Applying What You've Learned....................... 249
Knowledge Quiz & Study Guide Answer Key............................... 251
    Part 1: Multiple-Choice Answers... 251
    Part 2: True or False Answers.. 252
    Part 3: Short Answer Explanations..252
    Part 4: Case Studies & Application Answers.................................... 253
        Scenario 1: The Borrowing Dilemma... 253
        Scenario 2: The Real Estate Investor... 253
        Scenario 3: The Retirement Planner..253
    Part 5: Action Plan—Applying What You've Learned....................... 254
Index.. 256
ABOUT THE AUTHOR... 260

1

The Pandemic Epiphany

How I Discovered The Perfect Portfolio™

> **per·fect**
> /ˈpərfək(t)/
> adjective
> having all the required or desirable elements, qualities, or characteristics; as good as it is possible to be
>
> **port·fo·li·o**
> /pôrtˈfōlēō/
> noun
> a range of investments held by a person or organization

It was March 2020. The world was shutting down. Cities turned into ghost towns, businesses shuttered, and the stock market tanked. I remember sitting in my home office, watching the S&P 500 plummet day after day, wiping out trillions of dollars in value. My own portfolio—built over decades—was bleeding. I had seen market crashes before, but this one felt different. The fear was palpable, not just in the financial markets, but in everyday life. People were panic-buying toilet paper, shelves at grocery stores were empty, and the phrase *"essential workers"* suddenly became part of our daily vocabulary.

For the first time in my career, I found myself questioning everything I had been taught about investing. I had spent 15 years as a financial advisor, guiding clients on "smart" investment decisions—diversification, dollar-cost averaging, and the so-called safety of 60/40 portfolios (60% stocks, 40% bonds). Yet, here I was, watching traditional strategies crumble under the weight of a crisis.

And then it hit me.

I needed a system that *thrived* in chaos—a portfolio that could generate wealth, protect assets, and minimize taxes, no matter what the economy threw our way.

The Breaking Point: A $400,000 Mistake

The realization wasn't just theoretical. It was personal.

I had a client—let's call him Joe. He was 62, recently retired, with a $4 million portfolio that we had carefully built over the years. Joe was living comfortably, drawing around $150,000 per year from his investments, while keeping his tax bill manageable.

Then the pandemic hit. In a panic, Joe called me.

"Should we sell?" he asked. His portfolio had dropped by nearly $1 million in just a few weeks. He was worried, and I could hear the fear in his voice.

I assured him, *"No, Joe, the market will recover. We've been through this before."*

But Joe didn't listen. He sold a huge chunk of his stocks at a loss, locking in nearly $400,000 in losses. And the worst part? Just months later, the market rebounded. By the end of 2020, the S&P 500 had gained over 16%, and Joe was left sitting on the sidelines, missing out on the recovery.

I realized then that the traditional buy-and-sell model was broken. The moment you *sell*, you trigger taxes and risk missing out on gains. But what if you never had to sell?

The Buy, Borrow, Die Revelation

I started researching how the ultra-wealthy managed their money. The answer was shockingly simple: *They never sell their assets.*

Instead of selling stocks, they borrowed against them.

Instead of selling real estate, they refinanced it.

Instead of cashing out on businesses, they structured their wealth in ways that allowed them to pass it on tax-free.

This was the essence of the **Buy, Borrow, Die** strategy.

The wealthy *buy* appreciating assets—stocks, real estate, businesses, precious metals, even cryptocurrency.

Then, instead of selling and triggering capital gains taxes, they *borrow* against those assets, using cheap, low-interest loans to fund their lifestyle.

And when they pass away, their heirs inherit everything *tax-free*, thanks to the stepped-up basis loophole.

This wasn't some loophole hidden in the fine print of the tax code—it was an open secret that billionaires had been using for decades. The problem? No one was teaching middle-class investors how to do the same.

I decided to change that.

Building The Perfect Portfolio™

Armed with this new knowledge, I restructured my own investments. I built what I now call *The Perfect Portfolio™*—a portfolio designed specifically for **Buy, Borrow, Die** investors.

Here's what it looks like:

1. Core Growth Stocks & ETFs (50%)

- Instead of picking individual stocks, I focused on broad market ETFs like **SPY (S&P 500 ETF)** and **VTI (Total Stock Market ETF)**.
- The goal? Own assets that consistently appreciate over time.
- I reinvested dividends to maximize compounding.

2. Real Estate (30%)

- I refinanced my primary home at **2.75%** (thanks to pandemic-era interest rates).
- I invested in rental properties, focusing on cash flow and tax advantages.
- Through depreciation, I legally offset thousands of dollars in taxable income.

3. Cryptocurrency & Alternative Assets (10%)

- Bitcoin, Ethereum, and gold became part of my long-term hedge against inflation.
- I learned how to stake crypto to earn passive income.

4. Tax-Free Investments (10%)

- **Municipal Bonds**: Tax-free interest, especially for high earners.
- **Roth IRAs & Backdoor Roth Conversions**: I maxed out contributions to grow tax-free forever.

With this new system in place, I no longer worried about market crashes. Instead of selling, I borrowed against my assets at **2-4% interest rates**, using the cash to reinvest or cover living expenses.

The Epiphany: Wealth is About Control, Not Just Growth

The pandemic taught me that financial freedom isn't about having the *biggest* portfolio. It's about having control over your assets, your taxes, and your future.

I used to believe that the only way to retire was to build a massive nest egg and slowly withdraw 4% per year. Now, I know there's a better way—one that allows you to **keep growing your wealth while living tax-free**.

This book will show you exactly how to do it.

2

Be S.M.A.R.T.

Strategies to Maximize Assets and Reduce Taxes

> **smart**
> /smärt/
> *adjective*
> having or showing a quick-witted intelligence

After the pandemic reshaped my thinking, I became obsessed with one question: **How do the rich not only build wealth but keep it?**

I had spent years helping families plan for retirement, but the truth was, most of those plans revolved around **working hard, saving diligently, and then paying an enormous amount in taxes.** That's the playbook the average American follows. The wealthy? They play a different game.

I needed a simple framework that anyone—regardless of their income level—could use to build and keep their wealth. That's how I created the **S.M.A.R.T. Strategy**, an easy-to-follow system designed to help you **Save More, Minimize Taxes, and Accelerate Returns.**

Let me break it down.

S – Start with the Right Accounts

Most people focus only on how much they earn and invest. But if you don't **put your money in the right accounts, you're losing thousands in taxes every year.**

Taxable vs. Tax-Advantaged Accounts

Imagine two people: **John and Sarah.**

- **John** invests in a taxable brokerage account. He buys stocks and ETFs. Every time he sells, he pays **15-20% in capital gains taxes** (or more if he's a high earner).
- **Sarah** invests in a Roth IRA and a 401(k). Her investments grow tax-free. When she retires, she pays **zero taxes** on her withdrawals.

Who do you think ends up wealthier?

What I Did Differently

- **Maxed Out My Roth IRA:** Even though I made too much for direct contributions, I used a **Backdoor Roth IRA** (a legal way for high-income earners to convert traditional IRA contributions into a Roth).
- **Maxed Out My 401(k):** In 2024, the contribution limit is **$23,000 ($30,500 if you're over 50).** Every dollar in a traditional 401(k) lowers my taxable income.
- **Health Savings Account (HSA):** The most **tax-efficient** account. Contributions are tax-free, investments grow tax-free, and withdrawals for medical expenses are tax-free.

💡 **Pro Tip:** If your company offers a **401(k) match,** contribute at least enough to get the full match. It's free money!

M – Minimize Taxes with Smart Investing

The rich don't just earn money—they know how to **keep it out of the IRS's hands.**

The $44,000 Tax Mistake

One of my clients, **Tom,** sold his stocks after a big gain in 2021. He had made about **$200,000 in profit** but didn't realize he triggered **short-term capital gains taxes (up to 37%!).**

His tax bill? **$44,000.**

Had he held the stocks for over a year, he would have only paid **15-20% in long-term capital gains taxes.**

Strategies the Wealthy Use

1. **Hold Investments for Over a Year** → **Long-term capital gains rates are lower** than short-term.
2. **Invest in ETFs Instead of Mutual Funds** → ETFs have lower capital gains distributions.
3. **Use Municipal Bonds ("Munis")** → Earn **tax-free interest** (great for high earners).
4. **Tax-Loss Harvesting** → If an investment loses money, sell it to offset taxable gains.

💡 **Pro Tip:** If you're in a high tax bracket, **focus on tax-efficient investments like ETFs, index funds, and municipal bonds.**

A – Asset Protection: Use Debt the Right Way

The middle class fears debt. The wealthy **use it to get richer.**

I used to think debt was bad. Then I learned about **"good debt" vs. "bad debt."**

Good Debt vs. Bad Debt

Good Debt	Bad Debt
Mortgage (low interest)	Credit Card Debt (20%+ APR)
Business Loans	Car Loans (Depreciating Asset)
Borrowing Against Investments	Personal Loans (High-Interest)

The wealthy **don't sell their assets—they borrow against them.**

How I Used Good Debt to My Advantage

1. **Refinanced My Home at 2.75%** → Instead of paying off my mortgage, I invested the money. The stock market returns **8-10% annually** on average, so I made more by investing.
2. **Used a HELOC (Home Equity Line of Credit)** → Borrowed at **4% interest** and invested in rental properties earning **8-12% returns.**
3. **Borrowed Against Stocks (Instead of Selling)** → Used a margin loan to reinvest at **2-4% interest rates.**

💡 **Pro Tip:** Instead of paying off a mortgage early, consider investing extra cash into **higher-return assets.**

R – Reinvest Profits and Compound Wealth

Albert Einstein called **compound interest the 8th wonder of the world**—he wasn't wrong.

The biggest mistake I see? People cashing out their gains **too early.**

Let's say you invested **$10,000 in the S&P 500** in 2000.

- If you left it alone, it would be worth over **$75,000** today.
- If you pulled money out, you lost **years of compounding growth.**

How to Supercharge Your Investments

- **Reinvest Dividends:** Instead of taking cash payouts, let them buy more shares.
- **Automate Your Investing:** Set up **monthly auto-investing** into ETFs or index funds.
- **Don't Chase the Market:** Stick to your plan—even when stocks crash.

💡 Pro Tip: **The longer you stay invested, the more wealth you build.** Time in the market is more important than timing the market.

T – Transfer Wealth Tax-Free

The wealthy think in **generations,** not just years.

I used to think estate planning was only for the ultra-rich. Then I learned that **without proper planning, your heirs could lose 40%+ of your wealth to taxes.**

How the Rich Pass Down Wealth Without Paying Taxes

1. **Stepped-Up Basis** → Heirs inherit assets at their current market value, avoiding capital gains taxes.
2. **Roth IRA Conversions** → Convert traditional IRAs to **Roth IRAs** (so heirs get tax-free money).
3. **Trusts** → Protect assets from estate taxes and legal issues.
4. **Life Insurance** → Death benefits are tax-free and can pass on generational wealth.

What I Did Differently

- **Bought a Whole Life Insurance Policy** → Instead of just leaving cash, I ensured my family gets a **tax-free** payout.

- **Set Up a Living Trust** → Avoids probate and ensures my wealth transfers **efficiently.**
- **Gave My Kids Stocks Instead of Cash** → They get long-term capital gains rates instead of high-income tax rates.

💡 **Pro Tip:** If you have **over $1 million in assets, consider an estate plan** to protect your wealth from excessive taxation.

The S.M.A.R.T. Formula in Action

Once I implemented these strategies, I saw **a massive difference in my net worth.**

1. **Saved over $30,000 in taxes per year** by using tax-advantaged accounts.
2. **Increased my portfolio growth rate** by reinvesting dividends and leveraging debt.
3. **Paid almost zero capital gains taxes** through tax-loss harvesting and long-term holding.
4. **Built generational wealth** by structuring my investments to pass down tax-free.

The truth is, **you don't have to be a billionaire to use these strategies.**

You just have to be **S.M.A.R.T.**

The next chapter will show you **what money really is**—and why most people misunderstand its true power.

3

What Is Money?

Is a Cow Money?

mon·ey
/ˈmənē/
noun
something generally accepted as a medium of exchange, a measure of value, or a means of payment

I used to think I understood money. I worked with it every day, helping clients invest, budget, and plan for retirement. But it wasn't until I had a conversation with my 10-year-old son during the pandemic that I realized just how *wrong* most people are about what money actually is.

It all started when he asked me, *"Dad, what is money?"*

I laughed. *"It's what we use to buy things."*

He frowned. *"But why does it have value?"*

That simple question sent me down a rabbit hole that changed the way I viewed wealth forever.

The Truth About Money

Most people think money is **paper bills, coins, or the numbers in their bank account.** But money is **none of those things.**

Money is just a tool—a means of exchange. It's a way to **store and transfer value.** But here's the thing: *money itself has no value.*

Think about it. A **$100 bill** is just a piece of paper. If you were stranded on an island, would you rather have **a stack of $100 bills** or **food, water, and shelter?**

This is where my son's question got interesting.

He asked, *"Could a cow be money?"*

And that's when I realized—yes, **a cow absolutely could be money.**

The History of Money: From Cows to Crypto

Money has taken many forms throughout history. Long before we had dollars, euros, or yen, people used **livestock, shells, salt, and even giant stones as currency.**

- **Cows as Money** → In ancient times, cattle were one of the earliest forms of currency. Why? Because they had **real value.** They provided **milk, meat, and labor.**
- **Salt as Money** → The word "salary" comes from **salarium**, the payment Roman soldiers received in **salt.** Salt was valuable because it preserved food.
- **Gold as Money** → Gold became money because it was **scarce, durable, and universally accepted.**
- **Paper Money & the Gold Standard** → For centuries, paper money was **backed by gold.** But in 1971, the U.S. government ended the gold standard, making the dollar a **fiat currency**—meaning it's backed by nothing but **trust in the government.**

Today, money is mostly **digital.** Over **92% of the world's currency** exists in electronic form—just numbers on a screen.

So, what does this mean for us?

The Problem With Today's Money

The moment I realized that **money isn't real**—that it's just a system of trust—I started asking a new question:

"If money isn't backed by gold, cows, or anything real, then what stops the government from printing unlimited amounts of it?"

The answer? Nothing.

Inflation: The Silent Wealth Killer

Every time the government prints more money, it **reduces the value of the money you already have.**

- In 1970, a gallon of gas cost **36 cents.**
- In 1990, it was **$1.12.**
- In 2024, it's over **$4.00 in many places.**

That's not because gas got scarcer—it's because **the value of the dollar dropped.**

The $100,000 Mistake

I had a client, **Mike,** who worked hard, saved diligently, and kept his money in a savings account earning **0.5% interest.**

The problem? Inflation in 2022 hit **8-9%.** That meant every year, his **savings lost purchasing power.**

If Mike had $100,000 in the bank, in **10 years,** that money would be worth the equivalent of **$60,000 or less.**

💡 **Pro Tip:** Keeping large amounts of cash in a savings account is a **guaranteed way to lose wealth.**

How the Rich Use Money Differently

Here's what changed my mindset: The rich don't **save** money—they **own assets.**

While the middle class holds **cash,** the wealthy hold:

- **Stocks & ETFs** → Companies that **increase in value over time.**
- **Real Estate** → Properties that **generate income and appreciate.**
- **Gold & Bitcoin** → Hard assets that **protect against inflation.**
- **Businesses** → Companies that **produce cash flow.**

This is the secret: **Money is only useful if you turn it into assets.**

If you hold cash, inflation eats away at it. But if you own assets, **your wealth grows over time.**

So, Is a Cow Money?

The answer is: **A cow can be money—but only if people agree that it has value.**

That's the thing about money—it's **only worth what people believe it's worth.**

A $100 bill is just paper. A Bitcoin is just digital code. A cow is just livestock.

The real question isn't *what is money?*—it's **how do you use money to create lasting wealth?**

That's what the rest of this book will teach you.

4

The Millionaire Next Door

Joe's Journey to $6 Million by Never Selling

mil·lion·aire
/ˌmilyəˈner, ˈmilyəˌner/
noun
a person whose assets are worth $1 million or more

J oe wasn't the kind of guy you'd expect to be rich.

He didn't wear designer suits, drive a flashy car, or brag about his portfolio at dinner parties. In fact, if you met him at a grocery store, you'd assume he was just another middle-class retiree, living off Social Security and a modest savings account.

But Joe was worth over **$6 million**. And the craziest part? **He never made more than $85,000 a year.**

How did he do it?

Joe cracked the wealth-building code that most people never figure out: **He never sold.**

The Ordinary Guy Who Became a Millionaire

I first met Joe in 2003 when he walked into my office looking for financial advice. He was 42 years old, married, and had two kids. He worked as an engineer, making a solid income, but nothing extraordinary.

Joe's goal was simple: **He wanted to retire early, live comfortably, and never worry about running out of money.**

But when I asked him about his investment strategy, he told me something that surprised me.

"I buy stocks and never sell them."

At first, I thought he was joking. Every investor I worked with was obsessed with **timing the market**—buying low, selling high, and trying to outsmart Wall Street. But Joe? He had a different philosophy.

"I don't care about stock prices. I just buy great companies and hold them forever."

The Power of Never Selling

Joe's strategy was painfully simple, yet incredibly effective.

1. **He invested consistently** → Every month, he put $1,000 into the stock market, no matter what.
2. **He focused on quality companies** → He bought stocks like **Apple, Microsoft, Coca-Cola, and Johnson & Johnson**—businesses that had been around for decades.
3. **He reinvested dividends** → Instead of cashing out, he let his money compound.
4. **He never sold, no matter what** → Not during the 2008 financial crisis, not when COVID crashed the market in 2020, not when people panicked over interest rates.

And the results?

- In 2003, Joe had **$50,000 invested** in stocks.
- By 2010, that number had grown to **$500,000**.
- By 2020, it had ballooned to **$3.5 million**.
- Today, Joe's portfolio is worth over **$6 million**.

All because **he never sold.**

The $1,000 Decision That Changed His Life

Joe's secret wasn't luck—it was consistency.

In 2003, he bought **$1,000 worth of Apple stock**. At the time, Apple was trading at **$0.23 per share (split-adjusted).**

- **Today, that same $1,000 investment is worth over $450,000.**
- **If he had sold early, he would have missed out on millions.**

And Apple wasn't his only winner. Joe's portfolio was filled with companies that **compounded year after year.**

💡 **Pro Tip:** The biggest mistake most investors make is selling too soon. The best stocks keep growing over decades.

Why Most People Fail at Investing

Most people lose money in the stock market not because they pick bad stocks, but because they **can't sit still.**

They panic when the market drops.
They try to time the highs and lows.
They get impatient and sell early.

Joe never did any of that.

He ignored the headlines, the doomsday predictions, and the endless chatter about recessions. He understood that **real wealth comes from holding assets long-term.**

And guess what? Joe's approach is the **same strategy used by billionaires.**

- **Warren Buffett:** *"Our favorite holding period is forever."*
- **Jeff Bezos:** *"We're long-term thinkers. We don't worry about short-term stock prices."*

The difference? Most people **don't have the patience to stick with it.**

Joe's Three Rules for Becoming a Millionaire

Before he retired, I asked Joe to share his best advice. His response?

"Wealth isn't about making the right trades—it's about making the right habits."

Here are his **three rules for financial freedom:**

1. Buy and Hold Forever

- Don't chase quick profits.
- Pick **great companies and hold them for decades.**
- Selling triggers taxes and kills long-term gains.

2. Never Panic When the Market Crashes

- **In 2008**, Joe's portfolio dropped by **40%.** He didn't sell.
- **In 2020**, when COVID hit, he lost **$1.2 million in a month.** He didn't sell.
- **By 2021**, he had made it all back—and then some.

3. Reinvest Dividends & Keep Buying

- Dividends are the **most powerful wealth-building tool.**
- Instead of taking cash, reinvest every dollar to buy more shares.
- If the market drops, buy more stocks at a discount.

Joe's Life Today: A $6 Million Retirement

Joe is **62 now.** He retired at **55,** owns his home outright, and lives off **his investments.**

But here's the kicker: **He still hasn't sold.**

Instead, he follows the **Buy, Borrow, Die** strategy:

- He **borrows against his portfolio at 3-4% interest** instead of selling and paying capital gains taxes.
- His investments keep growing, tax-free.
- When he passes away, his kids will inherit everything **without paying a dime in capital gains taxes.**

Joe **never made six figures.** He never owned a business. He never hit the lottery.

He simply **played the long game.**

And that's why he's **The Millionaire Next Door.**

The Lesson: You Can Do This Too

Joe's strategy isn't some secret only available to the ultra-wealthy. **Anyone can do this.**

1. **Invest consistently.**
2. **Buy and hold great companies.**
3. **Ignore market noise and never sell.**
4. **Reinvest your dividends.**
5. **Use leverage instead of selling when you need cash.**

That's it. That's the formula.

Most people spend their lives **chasing money.** But the truth is, wealth isn't about how much you make—it's about **how well you keep and grow what you have.**

Joe understood that. Now, you do too.

5

Avoiding "Dead Money"

Invest in The Five Pillars That Can Secure Loans

dead
/ded/
adjective
(of a piece of equipment) no longer functioning

Joe's story made me rethink everything I knew about money. He never sold his assets. He never panicked during market crashes. And yet, he still lived a life of complete financial freedom.

How?

Because he never held what I now call **"dead money."**

What Is Dead Money?

Dead money is any money that **doesn't grow, doesn't generate income, and can't be leveraged.**

Here's a simple example:

Imagine you have **$100,000** sitting in a savings account earning **0.5% interest.** Meanwhile, inflation is rising at **3-7% per year.**

Your **real purchasing power is shrinking.**

That's dead money.

Another example?

Your home equity. Most people celebrate when they pay off their mortgage early. But guess what? A fully paid-off home is just **dead equity** unless you're using it to create more wealth.

The key to becoming truly rich is making sure **every dollar is working for you**—either earning returns or acting as collateral for loans.

That's why I created the **Five Pillars of Borrowable Wealth.** These are the assets that banks, lenders, and even private financial institutions will gladly let you **borrow against**—so you never have to sell.

The Five Pillars of Borrowable Wealth

The rich don't just buy assets—they buy **leveraged assets.**

Here are the **five asset classes that banks love** and that can be used to borrow at ultra-low interest rates:

1. Stocks & ETFs (Liquid Assets)

- **Why it's valuable:** Banks allow investors to borrow against their brokerage accounts using **margin loans or securities-backed lines of credit (SBLOCs).**
- **How much you can borrow:** 50-70% of your stock portfolio's value.
- **Interest rates: 3-5%** (much lower than personal loans or credit cards).
- **Example:** If you have **$1 million in stocks**, you could borrow **$500,000 to $700,000** tax-free.

💡 **Pro Tip:** Instead of selling stocks and triggering capital gains taxes, use an SBLOC to pull out cash for investments, real estate, or emergencies.

2. Real Estate (Tangible, Income-Generating Asset)

- **Why it's valuable:** Real estate has built-in tax advantages, appreciates over time, and can be leveraged through **mortgages, HELOCs, and cash-out refinances.**
- **How much you can borrow:** Up to **80%** of your home's value through a **cash-out refinance or HELOC (home equity line of credit).**
- **Interest rates: 4-7%** (varies based on credit score and loan type).
- **Example:** If your home is worth **$500,000** and you owe **$200,000**, you can pull out **$200,000+ in tax-free cash** to reinvest elsewhere.

💡 **Pro Tip:** The wealthy don't rush to pay off their mortgages. Instead, they refinance and use home equity to **buy more appreciating assets.**

3. Life Insurance (The Secret Loan Machine of the Rich)

- **Why it's valuable:** A properly structured **Indexed Universal Life (IUL) or Whole Life insurance policy** allows you to borrow against your cash value **without ever paying taxes.**
- **How much you can borrow: 90%** of your cash value.
- **Interest rates: 5-6%,** but your account still earns interest, making it a low-net-cost loan.
- **Example:** If you build up **$250,000** in cash value inside a policy, you could borrow **$225,000 tax-free** while your full balance keeps growing.

💡 **Pro Tip:** Banks recognize life insurance as a **safe asset**—many wealthy families use this strategy to fund investments and avoid estate taxes.

4. Businesses (The Most Overlooked Asset for Borrowing)

- **Why it's valuable:** A profitable business can secure **business lines of credit, SBA loans, and asset-backed financing**—without touching your personal assets.
- **How much you can borrow:** Banks typically lend **1-5x EBITDA (profit before taxes & expenses).**
- **Interest rates: 5-10%** depending on risk.
- **Example:** If your business earns **$200,000 in annual profits**, you may qualify for a **$400,000 to $1,000,000 loan** to expand operations or invest elsewhere.

💡 **Pro Tip:** Even small businesses can access loans and lines of credit. If you're self-employed, set up an **LLC or S-Corp** to leverage business lending options.

5. Precious Metals & Cryptocurrency (Alternative Borrowing Assets)

- **Why it's valuable: Gold, silver, and Bitcoin** can be used as collateral for loans, allowing investors to access cash without selling.
- **How much you can borrow:**
    - **Gold/Silver:** 50-75% of market value.
    - **Bitcoin/Ethereum:** 30-50% of market value (higher volatility).
- **Interest rates: 6-10%** (depends on lender and market conditions).
- **Example:** If you hold **$100,000 in Bitcoin**, some platforms will lend you **$30,000 to $50,000 tax-free.**

💡 **Pro Tip:** Instead of selling Bitcoin and paying **20-30% in taxes**, use crypto-backed lending platforms to borrow at **single-digit interest rates.**

Why This Matters: The Hidden Cost of Holding Dead Money

Case Study: The $500,000 Mistake

One of my clients, **Lisa**, had a fully paid-off home worth **$800,000.** She was proud of it. No mortgage, no debt—total peace of mind.

But here's the problem:

Her home equity was just **sitting there doing nothing.**

Meanwhile, she was watching inflation eat away at her cash savings, struggling to keep up with rising costs.

I showed her how to take out a **HELOC for $400,000 at 5% interest** and use that money to:

- Buy two rental properties that cash flowed **$3,000 per month**
- Invest in dividend-paying stocks generating **$20,000 per year**

Instead of holding **dead equity**, Lisa turned it into **income-producing assets.**

Within 5 years, her investments had grown by **$600,000,** while her debt was covered by cash flow.

💡 **Pro Tip:** A paid-off home sounds nice, but **leverage is what builds wealth.**

The rich don't keep **cash sitting in a bank account.** They use **other people's money (OPM)** to keep growing.

Now that you know **how the wealthy secure loans and build wealth**, the next chapter will show you how to **transform bad debt into good debt**—so you never get trapped by the wrong kind of borrowing.

6

Financial Alchemy

How to Transform "Bad Debt" into "Good Debt"

> **al·che·my**
> /ˈalkəmē/
> *noun*
> a process that is so effective that it seems like magic, such as the transformation of base metals into gold

Most people think all debt is bad. They've been told their whole lives to **pay off their mortgage early, avoid credit cards, and never take on loans unless absolutely necessary.**

But the wealthy? They don't just **use debt**—they turn it into a tool for building wealth.

That's **financial alchemy**: transforming **bad debt** (which drains your money) into **good debt** (which makes you richer).

The Two Types of Debt: Good vs. Bad

Not all debt is created equal. There's a **huge** difference between the type of debt that keeps people broke and the kind that creates millionaires.

Bad Debt (The Wealth Killer)

Bad debt is any loan that:

- **Charges high interest** (credit cards, payday loans).
- **Funds liabilities instead of assets** (financing vacations, buying a brand-new car).
- **Loses value over time** (personal loans for consumer goods).

📌 **Examples of Bad Debt:**

35

- **Credit Card Debt**: Average interest rate? **22-30%**. That means if you owe **$10,000**, you could pay **$2,000+ per year** in interest alone.
- **Car Loans**: The moment you drive off the lot, your car loses **10-20% of its value**. By the time you've paid it off, you've spent more in interest than the car is worth.
- **Personal Loans for Shopping**: Taking out a loan for **a luxury handbag or a new iPhone** is the fastest way to stay broke.

💡 **The Golden Rule of Bad Debt:** If it doesn't make you money, it's probably bad debt.

Good Debt (The Wealth Multiplier)

Good debt is any loan that:

- **Helps you buy appreciating assets** (real estate, stocks, businesses).
- **Has low interest rates** (mortgages, investment loans).
- **Can be used as leverage to grow wealth faster**.

📌 Examples of Good Debt:

- **Real Estate Loans**: A 30-year mortgage at **4-6% interest** is much cheaper than paying **100% cash** and losing liquidity.
- **Margin Loans (SBLOCs)**: Borrowing against stocks at **3-5% interest** to reinvest instead of selling.
- **Business Loans**: Using OPM (**Other People's Money**) to scale a business while keeping personal capital intact.

💡 **The Golden Rule of Good Debt:** If it makes you money, it's probably good debt.

Case Study: The $40,000 Mistake

One of my clients, **Mark**, had **$40,000 in savings** sitting in a bank account earning **0.5% interest**. Meanwhile, he was making **$900 monthly car payments** on a new **Mercedes-Benz**, with an interest rate of **7.5%**.

Here's the problem:

- His **car was losing value** every day.
- His savings were earning **less than inflation**.

Instead of **keeping dead money in the bank** while paying high interest, I helped Mark:
▪ Sell the luxury car and buy a **used, reliable car for $15,000**.

- Use **$25,000 from savings to invest in an income-producing rental property**.
- Leverage the property with a **3.5% fixed mortgage** (good debt).
- Earn **$1,500 per month in rental income**—which not only covered his **new car's costs** but also generated **extra cash flow.**

The result? In five years, that **$25,000 investment grew to $100,000** in home equity, while his car continued losing value.

💡 **Lesson:** The wealthy don't borrow money for liabilities. They borrow to **acquire assets that pay for their luxuries.**

How to Transform Bad Debt into Good Debt

If you're drowning in bad debt, don't panic—there's a way out.

Step 1: Refinance & Consolidate

The first step is **lowering your interest rates** and consolidating high-interest debt.

- **Balance Transfer Credit Cards** → If you have credit card debt, transfer it to a **0% interest card for 12-18 months**.
- **Personal Loan Consolidation** → Instead of paying **22-30% interest** on credit cards, take out a personal loan at **6-10% interest** and pay them off faster.
- **Refinance Auto Loans** → If your car loan is above **7% interest**, refinancing could save you thousands.

💡 **Pro Tip:** If your mortgage rate is above **6%**, consider refinancing when rates drop—your future self will thank you.

Step 2: Turn Liabilities into Income-Producing Assets

The goal isn't just to get rid of debt—it's to **use debt strategically to generate cash flow.**

Example 1: The Car Hack

- Instead of **financing a $60,000 car at 8%**, buy a **$20,000 car in cash** and invest the other **$40,000 in dividend stocks**.
- Your dividend yield at **4%** could pay for maintenance and insurance!

Example 2: House Hacking

- Buy a **duplex or triplex** with a low-down-payment mortgage.
- Rent out the other units—your tenants **pay your mortgage** while you build equity.

💡 **Pro Tip:** If you're a first-time homebuyer, check out **FHA Loans**—you can buy a house with **just 3.5% down.**

Step 3: Leverage Debt to Invest (Safely)

Once your debt is under control, you can **use good debt to grow your wealth faster.**

Smart Ways to Leverage Debt

- **HELOC (Home Equity Line of Credit):** Use equity in your home to invest in real estate, stocks, or a business.
- **SBLOC (Securities-Based Line of Credit):** Borrow against your brokerage account **instead of selling stocks and triggering taxes**.
- **Real Estate Syndications:** Pool your money with other investors and buy large properties without needing millions upfront.

💡 **Pro Tip:** Always ensure your **investment returns are higher than your borrowing costs.**

The $6 Million Strategy: How the Rich Use Debt to Build Wealth

The wealthy use a **3-step cycle** to keep getting richer without paying taxes:

1️⃣ **Buy Assets with Borrowed Money** → Use mortgages, margin loans, and business credit to acquire **income-generating assets**.
2️⃣ **Let Assets Appreciate** → Hold stocks, real estate, and businesses **long-term** while they grow.
3️⃣ **Borrow Against the Growth (Instead of Selling)** → When you need cash, take out **low-interest loans** against your assets instead of selling and paying capital gains taxes.

📌 **Example: The Buy, Borrow, Die Strategy in Action**

- John owns **$5 million in real estate** and **$2 million in stocks**.
- Instead of selling, he **borrows $500,000 at 3.5% interest** to fund his lifestyle.

- He never sells, never triggers capital gains, and never pays income tax on borrowed money.

When John passes away, his heirs get his **$7 million in assets tax-free** (thanks to the stepped-up basis rule).

💡 **The Lesson?** The wealthy **never sell. They borrow.**

Final Thoughts: Turning Debt into a Wealth-Building Tool

If you're still treating debt like a burden, it's time to **change your mindset**.

■ **Bad debt** keeps you poor. It funds liabilities.
■ **Good debt** makes you rich. It funds assets.
■ **Smart leverage** lets you grow wealth while keeping taxes low.

If you learn how to **transform bad debt into good debt**, you'll never fear borrowing money again—you'll use it as a **powerful wealth-building tool.**

The next chapter will show you **how to use stocks and ETFs—the first pillar of Buy, Borrow, Die—to create unstoppable wealth.**

PART ONE

Stocks and ETFs

The First Pillar of a Buy, Borrow, Die Strategy

The Five Pillars

When I first started investing, I did what everyone told me to do: **buy stocks, watch the market, and sell when prices went up.** It made sense at the time—buy low, sell high, and lock in your profits.

But after years of watching the ultra-wealthy manage their money, I realized something crucial:

They don't sell.

Instead of cashing out, they **borrow against their investments, let them keep growing, and pass them down tax-free.**

This is the foundation of the **Buy, Borrow, Die strategy**, and it all starts with the **first pillar: Stocks and ETFs.**

7

Buy Low and Never Sell

If you want to build **generational wealth**, the most important lesson you can learn is this:

The longer you hold stocks, the wealthier you become.

📌 Consider this: If you invested **$1,000 in the S&P 500 in 1980,** today that money would be worth over **$100,000**—and that's without adding a single extra dollar.

Why Most Investors Fail

The average investor doesn't get these returns because they **panic, sell too early, or try to time the market.**

I've seen it happen over and over again.

- **In 2008**, people sold their stocks after the market crashed, locking in their losses.
- **In 2020**, when COVID hit, investors sold in fear, only to watch the market recover **within months.**
- **In 2022**, rising interest rates scared people into selling, but by 2023, the market was already rebounding.

The wealthy? They held on. They **bought more during the crash** and rode the wave back up.

💡 **Lesson:** The stock market is a wealth-building machine—but only if you stay in it long enough.

Stocks and ETFs: The First Pillar of Buy, Borrow, Die

Why Stocks & ETFs Are the Best Wealth-Building Tool

- **They appreciate over time** (historically **8-10% per year**).
- **They pay dividends** (providing passive income).
- **They are liquid** (you can borrow against them easily).
- **They can be passed down tax-free** (via the stepped-up basis).

Instead of trading stocks, **buy them and hold them forever.**

📌 **Example: Warren Buffett's Strategy**
Buffett bought **$1 billion of Coca-Cola stock** in the 1980s. He's never sold. Today, it pays him **$700 million in annual dividends.**

That's how the rich get richer—they let **time and compounding do the work.**

What Should You Invest In?

1. S&P 500 ETFs (The No-Brainer Investment)

If you don't want to research individual stocks, just invest in the **S&P 500**.

Best ETFs:

- **SPY** (S&P 500 ETF)
- **VOO** (Vanguard S&P 500 ETF)
- **IVV** (iShares S&P 500 ETF)

Why?

- **Diversification:** Own 500 of America's best companies.
- **Consistent Growth:** Historically returns **8-10% per year.**
- **Low Fees:** No expensive management costs.

💡 **Pro Tip:** If you put **$500 per month into an S&P 500 ETF**, in 30 years, you'll have over **$1.5 million.**

2. Dividend Stocks (Get Paid While You Hold)

Dividend stocks are **the secret to creating passive income.**

Top Dividend Stocks:

- **Johnson & Johnson (JNJ)** → Pays a **2.5% annual dividend**
- **Coca-Cola (KO)** → Pays a **3% annual dividend**
- **Procter & Gamble (PG)** → Pays a **2.4% annual dividend**

📌 **Example: The $1,000,000 Dividend Plan**
If you invest **$1 million into dividend stocks paying 4%**, you'll receive **$40,000 per year—without selling a single share.**

3. Growth Stocks (High Risk, High Reward)

Growth stocks don't pay dividends, but they **explode in value over time.**

Top Growth Stocks:

- **Amazon (AMZN)** → Grew **50x in 20 years**
- **Tesla (TSLA)** → Turned **$10,000 into $1 million in a decade**
- **Apple (AAPL)** → Up **20,000% since 1980**

💡 **Pro Tip:** Invest **80% in safe stocks (ETFs, dividends) and 20% in high-growth stocks** for the best balance of safety and upside.

How to Borrow Against Your Stocks (Instead of Selling)

Once you've built a portfolio, you **never need to sell your stocks to access cash.** Instead, you can **borrow against them using a securities-backed line of credit (SBLOC).**

How SBLOCs Work

- **You can borrow up to 70% of your portfolio's value.**
- **Low interest rates (3-5%)** compared to credit cards (20%+).
- **No capital gains taxes** because you're not selling.

📌 **Example: Using an SBLOC Instead of Selling**

- You own **$500,000 in stocks.**

- You borrow **$250,000 at 4% interest** instead of selling.
- Your **stocks keep growing**, and you pay back the loan with dividends or investment gains.

💡 **Lesson:** Borrowing against your assets keeps your wealth compounding—while letting you live off your money tax-free.

How the Buy, Borrow, Die Strategy Works with Stocks

Let's say you build a **$5 million stock portfolio** over your lifetime.

Step 1: Buy and Hold

- Invest in ETFs, dividend stocks, and growth companies.
- Let your portfolio grow **8-10% per year**.

Step 2: Borrow Instead of Selling

- Need money? Borrow **$250,000 tax-free at 3-4% interest** instead of selling.
- Your portfolio keeps compounding, and you never trigger capital gains taxes.

Step 3: Pass It Down Tax-Free

- When you pass away, your heirs inherit the **full $5 million portfolio tax-free** (thanks to the stepped-up basis).
- They continue borrowing against it, keeping the cycle going.

📌 **Example: The Rockefeller Strategy**
The **Rockefellers never sell their assets.** Instead, they borrow against them, reinvest, and pass them down **generation after generation—without paying taxes.**

This is **exactly** how the ultra-rich stay rich.

Now that you understand the power of stocks and ETFs, the next chapter will show you **how to use fear and greed to amplify your returns—so you can grow wealth even faster.**

8

Stocks and ETFs

The Good, the Bad, and the Ugly

> **stock**
> /stäk/
> *noun*
> part of the ownership of a company that can be bought by members of the public

Stocks and ETFs are the **cornerstone** of the **Buy, Borrow, Die strategy**—but not all stocks are created equal.

Some are **long-term wealth builders** that make millionaires.
Some are **overhyped time bombs** that crash overnight.
And some are just **outright scams.**

Knowing the difference between **good, bad, and ugly investments** is what separates **the wealthy from the broke.**

The Good: Wealth-Building Stocks & ETFs

Let's start with the best investments—the ones that build **real, lasting wealth.**

These are **stocks and ETFs that:** ■ **Appreciate over time** (10+ years of consistent growth).
■ **Pay dividends** (providing passive income).
■ **Are essential to the economy** (companies that will be around in 50 years).
■ **Let you borrow against them** (used as collateral for loans).

1. S&P 500 ETFs (The Easiest Path to Wealth)

If you only invest in one thing, make it an **S&P 500 ETF**.

📌 **Best ETFs:**

- **SPY** (State Street S&P 500 ETF)
- **VOO** (Vanguard S&P 500 ETF)
- **IVV** (iShares S&P 500 ETF)

💡 **Why?**

- **Historical 8-10% annual returns** (better than 99% of hedge funds).
- **Owns 500+ of America's best companies** (Apple, Microsoft, Amazon, etc.).
- **Zero effort**—just buy and let it grow.

📌 **Example:**
If you invest **$1,000/month in SPY** starting at age 25, you'll have **$2.3 million by age 65**.

2. Dividend Stocks (Get Paid While You Hold)

Dividend stocks **pay you cash every quarter**, whether the market goes up or down.

📌 **Best Dividend Stocks:**

- **Johnson & Johnson (JNJ)** → 2.5% annual dividend
- **Coca-Cola (KO)** → 3% annual dividend
- **Procter & Gamble (PG)** → 2.4% annual dividend

📌 **Example:**
If you invest **$500,000 in dividend stocks averaging 4% dividends**, you'll receive **$20,000 per year in passive income**—without selling a single share.

---

3. Blue-Chip Stocks (Boring but Safe)

These are **rock-solid companies** that have survived recessions, wars, and market crashes.

📌 **Best Blue-Chip Stocks:**

- **Apple (AAPL)** → Dominates tech, pays dividends.

- **Microsoft (MSFT)** → Cloud computing & AI leader.
- **Berkshire Hathaway (BRK.B)** → Warren Buffett's empire.

💡 Why?

- These companies don't go bankrupt.
- They grow consistently over **decades**.
- They make great collateral for loans (SBLOCs).

The Bad: Overhyped & Risky Stocks

Some stocks **look** like great investments but have serious red flags.

1. Meme Stocks (Short-Term Hype, Long-Term Disaster)

GameStop, AMC, and Bed Bath & Beyond are **great for traders but terrible for investors.**

📌 Why Avoid?
❌ **No real earnings growth.**
❌ **Massive volatility—up 300% one day, down 80% the next.**
❌ **Retail investors get burned while hedge funds profit.**

💡 **Lesson:** If you're investing, not trading, **ignore meme stocks.**

2. SPACs & Penny Stocks (99% Crash to Zero)

Special Purpose Acquisition Companies (SPACs) and penny stocks **promise huge returns—but most end in disaster.**

📌 Red Flags:
❌ **Companies with no revenue but billion-dollar valuations.**
❌ **CEO is a Twitter influencer hyping the stock.**
❌ **Trading below $5 per share (penny stock territory).**

📌 Example:
Nikola (NKLA) went public at **$30 per share**, hit **$90 per share**, then crashed to **$1.50** after it was exposed as a fraud.

💡 **Lesson:** If a stock sounds too good to be true, it probably is.

3. High-Fee Mutual Funds (The Hidden Wealth Killer)

Most mutual funds **underperform the market** while charging **high fees**.

📌 **Why Avoid?**
❌ Expense ratios of 1-2% eat your profits.
❌ Most fail to beat the S&P 500 over time.
❌ You're better off in low-cost ETFs.

💡 **Pro Tip:** Always check the **expense ratio** before investing. Anything above **0.5% is too high**.

The Ugly: Stocks That Destroy Wealth

Now let's talk about the worst investments—the ones that **wipe out entire portfolios**.

1. Companies That Go Bankrupt

Just because a company is famous **doesn't mean it will survive**.

📌 **Examples of Famous Companies That Went Bankrupt:**

- **Blockbuster (2000s)** → Ignored Netflix, died.
- **Sears (2018)** → Once the largest retailer in the U.S., now gone.
- **Lehman Brothers (2008)** → A top investment bank, wiped out in the financial crisis.

💡 **Lesson:** If a company is **bleeding money and losing market share**, don't assume it will recover.

2. IPOs (The Hype Trap)

Most Initial Public Offerings (IPOs) **make insiders rich while leaving investors broke**.

📌 **Example: Facebook vs. Snapchat**

- **Facebook IPO (2012):** Priced at **$38 per share**, crashed to **$18**, but then grew **over 1,000%**.
- **Snapchat IPO (2017):** Launched at **$27 per share**, now worth **$9 per share**.

💡 **Lesson:** Avoid IPOs until the **hype settles and real earnings emerge**.

3. Fraudulent Stocks (The Next Enron)

Some companies **cook their books and deceive investors**—until it all collapses.

📌 **Biggest Corporate Frauds in History:**

- **Enron (2001):** Faked earnings, wiped out $60 billion in investor wealth.
- **Theranos (2018):** Promised breakthrough medical tech—was a total scam.
- **FTX (2022):** Claimed to be the safest crypto exchange—stole billions.

💡 **Lesson:** If a company's profits seem **too good to be true**, they probably are.

Final Thoughts: How to Build the Perfect Stock Portfolio

■ **80% Safe Investments:**

- S&P 500 ETFs (SPY, VOO, IVV)
- Dividend Stocks (JNJ, KO, PG)
- Blue-Chip Stocks (AAPL, MSFT, BRK.B)

■ **20% Growth & Risky Plays:**

- Tech Leaders (GOOGL, TSLA, NVDA)
- High-growth stocks (but not meme stocks)

🚫 **Avoid:**
❌ Meme stocks
❌ Penny stocks & SPACs
❌ High-fee mutual funds
❌ Hype-based IPOs

The secret to **Buy, Borrow, Die** isn't gambling on stocks—it's **buying great companies and never selling.**

In the next chapter, I'll show you **how to use fear and greed to make smarter investment decisions—so you can grow wealth faster than the average investor.**

9

Buy More and Never Sell

Using Fear and Greed to Amplify Your Returns

In the world of investing, there are two emotions that drive every decision—**fear and greed**.

These emotions are responsible for every stock market crash, every irrational rally, and every investment mistake people make.

But here's the thing:

If you learn to control fear and greed, you can use them to your advantage—and make millions in the process.

The Secret of the 1%: Buy More When Others Are Afraid

Most investors panic when the stock market drops.

They see their portfolio in the red and think, *"I need to sell before I lose everything."*

But the wealthy? They see **opportunity** where others see disaster.

> 📌 **Example: Warren Buffett's Golden Rule**
> *"Be fearful when others are greedy, and greedy when others are fearful."*

This simple philosophy is why Buffett **buys stocks during every major crash**—while average investors run for the exits.

> 💡 **Lesson:** The best time to buy stocks isn't when everything looks great—it's when everyone else is panicking.

How Fear Creates the Best Buying Opportunities

Every time the stock market crashes, people assume it's different this time. But the truth is, **the market always recovers**—and those who buy during the panic make the most money.

📌 **The Best Buying Opportunities in Recent History:**

Crash	Market Drop	Recovery Time	Profit if You Bought at the Bottom
2008 Financial Crisis	-50%	3 years	+400% (S&P 500 2009-2021)
2020 COVID Crash	-34%	6 months	+120% (S&P 500 2020-2021)
2022 Tech Crash	-30% (NASDAQ)	1 year	+50% (2023-2024)

Case Study: The $100,000 Decision That Made $1 Million

I had a client, **Dan**, who had **$100,000 in cash** waiting to invest. In March 2020, when COVID crashed the market, I told him, *"Now is the time to buy."*

He was terrified. *"What if the market keeps crashing?"*

But I convinced him to **buy $100,000 of S&P 500 ETFs (SPY) at $220 per share.**

By the end of 2021, SPY had rebounded to **$470 per share—more than doubling his money in less than two years.**

Today, his portfolio is worth over **$1 million**, all because he bought during peak fear.

💡 **Lesson:** The best opportunities come when **everyone is afraid**—but only those who act on it get rich.

How to Profit From Greed Without Getting Burned

While fear creates **buying opportunities, greed creates bubbles.**

When people see stocks rising fast, they start thinking, *"I can't miss out on this!"*—and they rush in **at the worst time.**

📌 **The Most Famous Greed-Driven Bubbles:**

- **1999 Dot-Com Bubble:** People bought tech stocks with no earnings → Market crashed **80%**.

- **2008 Housing Bubble:** Everyone thought real estate would never go down → Banks collapsed.
- **2021 Meme Stock Mania:** AMC, GameStop, Dogecoin → Many lost **90%+ of their money.**

Case Study: The $50,000 Mistake

In 2021, my friend **Tom** saw Tesla skyrocketing.

It had already gone up **700%** in two years, but he didn't want to miss out.

So, he **bought $50,000 of Tesla at $1,200 per share.**

By 2022, Tesla crashed to **$600 per share**—wiping out **half his investment.**

Had he waited for a **dip during market fear**, he could have **bought at a much lower price and doubled his profits.**

💡 **Lesson:** When everyone is greedy, slow down. **Patience beats FOMO every time.**

How to Use Fear & Greed to Make More Money

Step 1: Buy More When Fear Peaks

- If the market drops **20% or more**, it's a buying opportunity.
- Look at **historical crashes**—the market always recovers.
- Use **cash reserves or a margin loan** to buy cheap stocks.

📌 **Example:** If you had bought during the 2022 crash, you'd be up **50% today.**

Step 2: Take Profits When Greed Peaks

- If stocks **skyrocket too fast**, consider **taking partial profits**.
- If people who never invest suddenly start giving stock advice—be careful.
- Move some gains into safer assets like **dividend stocks or real estate.**

📌 **Example:** If you had **sold meme stocks at their peak in 2021**, you could have **saved 90% of your money.**

Step 3: Never Sell Your Core Portfolio—Borrow Instead

Instead of selling stocks when you need cash, **use an SBLOC (Securities-Based Line of Credit).**

- Borrow **50-70% of your stock portfolio at 3-5% interest**.
- Avoid capital gains taxes.
- Keep your investments growing long-term.

📌 **Example:** If you have **$500,000 in stocks**, you can borrow **$250,000 tax-free** without selling.

Final Thoughts: How to Become a Master Investor

■ Use fear to buy more when stocks are cheap.
■ Use greed as a warning sign to take profits.
■ Never sell your core assets—borrow instead.
■ Remember: Time in the market beats timing the market.

The **wealthy don't sell their investments—they buy more when others panic.**

Now that you understand how to **control fear and greed to maximize profits**, the next chapter will show you **how Buy, Borrow, Die is truly for everyday Americans—not just billionaires.**

10

Buy, Borrow, Die

It Really Is for Everyday Americans

For years, I thought the **Buy, Borrow, Die** strategy was only for billionaires.

I assumed it was a loophole used by hedge fund managers, tech CEOs, and Wall Street insiders—the kind of people who had family offices and private wealth advisors.

But then I realized something that changed everything:

Anyone—yes, even everyday Americans—can use this strategy to build tax-free wealth.

This isn't just for the ultra-rich. **If you own a home, invest in stocks, or have a retirement account, you can use Buy, Borrow, Die to create generational wealth.**

Let me show you how.

Why Buy, Borrow, Die Works for Everyone

Step 1: Buy Appreciating Assets

The first step is **owning the right kind of assets**—ones that increase in value over time.

- ■ **Stocks & ETFs** → Grow **8-10% per year** on average.
- ■ **Real Estate** → Home values double every **10-15 years**.
- ■ **Business Ownership** → Can generate passive income and tax benefits.

💡 **The Key:** Instead of focusing on **cash**, focus on **assets that grow**.

Step 2: Borrow Against Those Assets (Instead of Selling)

Once your assets grow, you'll need money to fund your lifestyle, invest, or cover expenses.

Most people sell their assets—but that triggers taxes.

Instead, the rich **borrow against their assets** at low interest rates.

📌 How Everyday Americans Can Borrow Against Assets:

Asset Type	Loan Type	Loan-to-Value (LTV)	Interest Rate
Stocks & ETFs	SBLOC (Securities-Based Line of Credit)	50-70%	3-5%
Real Estate	HELOC (Home Equity Line of Credit)	75-80%	4-7%
Life Insurance	Policy Loan	90% of cash value	5-6%

📌 Example:

- You own **$300,000 in stocks** → Borrow **$150,000 tax-free**.
- You own **a home worth $500,000 with $200,000 in equity** → Borrow **$100,000 tax-free**.

💡 **Lesson:** By borrowing instead of selling, **your assets keep growing while you access cash.**

Step 3: Pass It Down Tax-Free

The final step is what makes **Buy, Borrow, Die the ultimate wealth-building strategy.**

Instead of ever selling assets, you **hold them until you die**—and when your heirs inherit them, they get a **stepped-up cost basis.**

■ **Your heirs don't pay capital gains taxes on the appreciation.**
■ **Your wealth gets passed down tax-free.**

📌 Example:

- You buy stocks worth **$100,000** and they grow to **$500,000** over your lifetime.
- If you sell, you owe **capital gains taxes** on $400,000.
- But if you pass them down, **your heirs inherit them tax-free** at the $500,000 value.

💡 **Lesson:** The tax code rewards people who **buy and hold forever.**

How Everyday Americans Can Use Buy, Borrow, Die

Case Study #1: The Middle-Class Homeowner

Sarah and Mike bought a home in **2010 for $250,000.**
By 2024, their home was worth **$600,000.**

Instead of selling, they **took out a $200,000 HELOC at 5% interest.**

- They used **$100,000 to invest in rental properties.**
- They used **$50,000 for home improvements.**
- They used **$50,000 to fund their retirement account.**

Their home continued appreciating while they **used borrowed money to create more wealth.**

💡 **Lesson:** Your home is more than just a place to live—it's an asset you can **leverage for tax-free cash.**

Case Study #2: The Everyday Investor

Joe, a school teacher, started investing in stocks at **30 years old.**

- He put **$500 per month into an S&P 500 ETF (VOO).**
- After 20 years, his portfolio grew to **$500,000.**
- Instead of selling, he **borrowed $250,000 using an SBLOC at 4% interest.**
- He reinvested the money into **dividend stocks paying 5% dividends.**
- His dividends **covered the loan payments, so he paid nothing out of pocket.**

💡 **Lesson:** You don't need to be rich—just consistent. Buy assets, borrow against them, and let **compound growth do the work.**

Case Study #3: The Retiree Who Pays No Taxes

David is **65 years old** and retired with a **$2 million stock portfolio.**

Instead of selling his stocks (which would trigger **capital gains taxes**), he **borrows $100,000 per year from his SBLOC.**

- ◼ No income tax, because loans aren't taxable.
- ◼ No capital gains tax, because he never sells.
- ◼ When he dies, his kids inherit his full portfolio tax-free.

💡 **Lesson:** Retirement planning isn't about withdrawing—it's about **leveraging assets tax-free.**

The Truth About Buy, Borrow, Die: It's Not Just for Billionaires

A lot of people hear about **Buy, Borrow, Die** and think it's only for the rich.

But here's the truth:

- If you own **stocks**, you can use an SBLOC.
- If you own **a home**, you can use a HELOC.
- If you have **life insurance**, you can borrow from it.

The key isn't being rich—it's **owning the right kind of assets.**

You don't need millions to start. Even if you only have **$50,000 in stocks or home equity,** you can **begin leveraging your assets now** and start compounding tax-free wealth.

How to Get Started with Buy, Borrow, Die

Step 1: Own Appreciating Assets

- Buy **stocks, ETFs, and real estate** that grow over time.
- Avoid **cash-heavy savings that lose value to inflation.**

Step 2: Use Smart Leverage

- Open an **SBLOC (Securities-Based Line of Credit)** if you have stocks.
- Use a **HELOC (Home Equity Line of Credit)** if you own a home.
- Borrow from your **life insurance policy** if you have whole life or IUL.

Step 3: Never Sell (Pass It Down Tax-Free)

- Borrow against assets instead of selling.
- Use **dividends, rental income, or business cash flow** to pay off debt.
- Pass down wealth to your kids **with a stepped-up cost basis.**

11

The Basics of Financial Alchemy

Press Buttons and Create Money!

If I told you that the wealthy have a way to **press a button and create money out of thin air**, would you believe me?

At first, I didn't either.

But after years of studying how the rich manage their wealth, I realized **they don't just earn money—they create it.**

Not by working harder.
Not by trading their time for dollars.
But by **turning assets into cash flow**—without selling anything.

This is what I call **Financial Alchemy**—the ability to transform **existing wealth into new wealth** without paying taxes, losing control, or depleting assets.

The Secret of the Wealthy: Money Isn't Earned—It's Created

Most people believe that **making more money** means working longer hours, getting a raise, or starting a side hustle.

But the rich don't think like that.

Instead of trading time for money, they **use leverage to multiply their existing wealth**—creating money out of nowhere.

Here's how they do it.

Step 1: Buy Assets That Appreciate

To create money, you first need **something valuable that grows over time.**

■ **Stocks & ETFs** → Grow 8-10% annually.
■ **Real Estate** → Property values double every 10-15 years.
■ **Business Ownership** → Produces cash flow & equity growth.
■ **Cryptocurrency & Gold** → Inflation hedges with high upside.

📌 **Example:**

- You invest **$100,000 in an S&P 500 ETF**.
- In 10 years, it's worth **$215,000** (assuming a 7.5% return).
- You didn't **work for this money**—the asset created it for you.

💡 **Lesson:** If you own appreciating assets, your money is **working for you 24/7.**

Step 2: Borrow Against Your Assets (Instead of Selling)

Here's where the magic happens.

Once you have assets, you don't need to sell them to access cash. **You can borrow against them tax-free.**

📌 **How the Wealthy Borrow Against Their Assets:**

Asset Type	Loan Type	Loan-to-Value (LTV)	Interest Rate
Stocks & ETFs	SBLOC (Securities-Based Line of Credit)	50-70%	3-5%
Real Estate	HELOC (Home Equity Line of Credit)	75-80%	4-7%
Life Insurance	Policy Loan	90% of cash value	5-6%

💡 **Why Borrowing Is Better Than Selling:**
■ **No capital gains taxes.**
■ **Your assets keep appreciating.**
■ **Interest rates are low (cheaper than credit cards & personal loans).**

📌 **Example:**

- You own **$500,000 in stocks**.
- Instead of selling, you **borrow $250,000 at 4% interest**.

- You use the money to **buy another appreciating asset** (real estate, stocks, or a business).
- Your **assets continue growing**, and you never pay taxes on the borrowed money.

💡 **Lesson:** The rich never sell assets—they use them as **collateral to create money.**

Step 3: Use New Money to Buy More Assets

Here's the real trick:

Instead of spending the borrowed money on liabilities (cars, vacations, shopping), the wealthy **use it to buy more assets.**

📌 **Example: The Infinite Money Loop**

- You own **$300,000 in stocks**.
- You borrow **$150,000 at 4%** and invest it in **a rental property**.
- The rental property generates **$1,500 per month** in income.
- You use the rent to **pay off the loan** while your stocks keep growing.
- Over time, both your **stocks and real estate** appreciate—creating wealth **out of thin air.**

💡 **Lesson:** The rich create money not by earning more—but by owning and borrowing strategically.

The Ultimate Trick: Using Debt to Pay for Your Lifestyle

Here's the part that blew my mind when I first learned it:

The ultra-wealthy don't sell investments to fund their lifestyle.
They borrow at low interest rates and live off tax-free debt.

📌 **Example: Jeff Bezos' Money Hack**

- Bezos owns **millions of Amazon shares** but rarely sells them.
- Instead, he **borrows billions** against his stock at ultra-low rates.
- He pays **zero income tax** because debt isn't taxable.

This means **he can live like a billionaire without ever triggering capital gains taxes.**

💡 **Lesson:** If you need cash, **borrow against assets instead of selling them.**

The Middle-Class Version: How Everyday People Can Use Financial Alchemy

This isn't just for billionaires—you can **start small and scale up.**

Case Study #1: The Homeowner's Money Machine

- **Lisa bought a home in 2010 for $250,000.**
- By 2024, it's worth **$600,000.**
- She takes out a **$150,000 HELOC** and buys **two rental properties.**
- The rental income covers the loan, and she builds **$300,000 in new real estate wealth.**

💡 **Lesson:** A home isn't just a place to live—it's **leverage to create more wealth.**

Case Study #2: The Everyday Investor's Money Button

- **Joe has $100,000 in an S&P 500 ETF (VOO).**
- He borrows **$50,000 from an SBLOC** at **4% interest.**
- He reinvests in **high-dividend stocks paying 5%.**
- The dividends **cover the loan interest** while his portfolio keeps growing.

💡 **Lesson:** If your assets earn more than your loan interest, you've created free money.

💡 **The secret of Financial Alchemy is simple:**

- **Press a button (borrow money).**
- **Use it to buy appreciating assets.**
- **Let those assets grow.**
- **Repeat the process forever.**

That's how you **create money out of thin air—without ever working harder.**

The next chapter will show you **how to turn bad debt into good debt—so you can build wealth even faster.**

12

IRA

It IS a Retirement Account! (so Focus on Your Financial Independence)

For decades, Americans have been told that **an IRA (Individual Retirement Account) is the smartest way to save for retirement.**

And for the most part, that's true.

An IRA is one of the **most powerful tax-advantaged accounts available**, allowing everyday investors to **grow their money tax-free or tax-deferred**—depending on the type of IRA they choose.

But here's the problem: **Most people don't use IRAs correctly.**

They either:
✘ **Don't contribute enough** to maximize the benefits.
✘ **Ignore the tax advantages** and withdraw early (losing money to penalties).
✘ **Forget that IRAs can be used** as investment accounts, not just savings accounts.

In this chapter, I'll show you **why an IRA is a retirement account**, how to use it **the right way**, and why **it's one of the best tools for building tax-free wealth.**

What Is an IRA, Really?

An **IRA is not just a savings account—it's a powerful investment vehicle.**

There Are Two Main Types of IRAs:

IRA Type	Tax Treatment	Best For
Traditional IRA	Contributions are tax-deductible, but withdrawals are taxed in retirement.	People who expect to be in a **lower tax bracket in retirement.**
Roth IRA	Contributions are after-tax, but withdrawals are **100% tax-free** in retirement.	People who want **tax-free growth and withdrawals.**

📌 **Key IRA Rules (2024):**

- Contribution limit: **$7,000 per year** ($8,000 if 50+).
- You must have **earned income** to contribute.
- **Early withdrawals before age 59½ trigger a 10% penalty** (unless using a qualified exception).

💡 **Lesson:** An IRA isn't just a place to park money—it's a tax-advantaged way to **grow wealth.**

How to Maximize Your IRA for Retirement

Step 1: Choose the Right Type of IRA

Before contributing, ask yourself:

- **Do I want a tax break now (Traditional IRA) or tax-free withdrawals later (Roth IRA)?**

📌 **Rule of Thumb:**

- If you expect to be in a **lower tax bracket in retirement**, choose a **Traditional IRA** for **upfront tax savings.**
- If you expect to be in a **higher tax bracket later**, choose a **Roth IRA** so your withdrawals are **100% tax-free.**

Step 2: Invest for Growth, Not Just Safety

Many people treat their IRA like a **bank savings account**, keeping their money in **low-yield investments**.

✖ Bad IRA Investments:

- Cash (0% return).
- Low-yield bonds (2-3% return).

■ Good IRA Investments:

- **S&P 500 ETFs (SPY, VOO, IVV)** → Average **8-10% annual growth.**
- **Dividend Stocks (JNJ, KO, PG)** → Passive income + growth.
- **Growth Stocks (AAPL, MSFT, NVDA)** → High potential over decades.

📌 Example:

- If you invest **$7,000 per year** in an **S&P 500 ETF** inside your IRA, after **30 years**, you'll have **$1.1 million tax-free (Roth) or tax-deferred (Traditional).**

💡 **Lesson:** An IRA is **not a savings account—it's an investment account.**

Step 3: Max Out Contributions Every Year

Most people **don't contribute enough** to take full advantage of an IRA.

📌 Why maxing out is crucial:

- You can't go back and contribute for past years—**once the year is over, the opportunity is gone.**
- The earlier you invest, the more **compound interest** works in your favor.

📌 Example:

- **John contributes $7,000 per year from age 25 to 35** → Stops investing.
- **Sarah contributes $7,000 per year from age 35 to 65** → 30 years of investing.
- **Who ends up with more money at 65? John—because he started earlier!**

💡 **Lesson:** The earlier you contribute, the **less money you need to invest** to reach the same goal.

Step 4: Avoid Early Withdrawals (Unless Absolutely Necessary)

One of the biggest mistakes IRA holders make is **withdrawing money too soon**—triggering **penalties and taxes.**

📌 **What Happens If You Withdraw Early?**
❌ 10% penalty **before age 59½.**
❌ Pay income tax on withdrawals (Traditional IRA).

📌 **Exceptions Where You Can Withdraw Early (Penalty-Free):**
▪ First-time home purchase (up to $10,000).
▪ Qualified education expenses.
▪ Medical expenses or disability.

💡 **Lesson: Don't touch your IRA unless it's a true emergency**—it's meant for retirement, not short-term spending.

Step 5: Convert a Traditional IRA to a Roth IRA for Tax-Free Retirement

One of the biggest secrets to **tax-free wealth** is the **Roth IRA conversion.**

📌 **Why Convert?**

- Traditional IRAs require **taxes on withdrawals.**
- A Roth IRA lets your money **grow tax-free forever.**

📌 **How It Works:**

- Convert **some or all of your Traditional IRA into a Roth IRA.**
- Pay taxes on the converted amount **now, at today's tax rates.**
- All future withdrawals are **100% tax-free.**

💡 **Pro Tip:** Convert **small amounts each year** to avoid getting pushed into a higher tax bracket.

💡 **The Lesson?**

An IRA is **one of the best retirement tools available**—but only if you use it correctly.

The next chapter will challenge everything you just learned, as we explore why **an IRA might NOT actually be a retirement account**... and why you should think of it differently.

13

Future-Proof Your Savings:

Borrow to Fund the Tax Benefits of a Roth IRA

Most people assume that **you need cash on hand to max out your Roth IRA** every year.

That's not true.

The wealthy have a trick—they **borrow strategically to fund their tax-free Roth IRA contributions.**

Yes, you read that right.

You can use leverage to supercharge your Roth IRA, ensuring you never miss a year of tax-free growth—even if you don't have the cash available today.

This is one of the **most overlooked wealth-building strategies**, and if you use it correctly, it can put you years ahead of the average investor.

Why Funding Your Roth IRA Every Year Is Crucial

The IRS limits how much you can put into a Roth IRA each year.

📌 **2024 Roth IRA Contribution Limits:**

- **$7,000 per year** ($8,000 if you're 50+).

Once the year is over, **you can't go back and contribute for missed years.**

💡 **The Secret?** If you miss contributions today, you're leaving **decades of tax-free compound growth on the table.**

Step 1: Use Low-Interest Borrowing to Fund Your Roth IRA

If you don't have extra cash, you can **borrow at low interest rates and invest the money into a Roth IRA.**

Since a Roth IRA grows **100% tax-free**, the returns often **outpace the borrowing cost.**

📌 **Where to Borrow From to Fund Your Roth IRA:**

Loan Type	Best For	Interest Rate
HELOC (Home Equity Line of Credit)	Homeowners with equity	4-7%
SBLOC (Securities-Based Line of Credit)	Investors with stock portfolios	3-5%
0% APR Credit Cards (12-18 months)	Short-term borrowing	0% (intro rate)
Margin Loan from Brokerage Account	Experienced investors	4-6%

📌 **Example:**

- You take out a **$7,000 loan from a HELOC at 5% interest.**
- You invest it in a **Roth IRA ETF (SPY, VOO)** averaging 8-10% annual returns.
- Your Roth IRA grows tax-free, while your **investment return covers the loan interest.**

💡 **Lesson:** If your **Roth IRA return (8-10%) is greater than your borrowing cost (3-5%),** you're creating **free wealth.**

Step 2: Invest the Roth IRA in High-Growth Assets

If you're using leverage to fund your Roth IRA, you need **investments that grow faster than your borrowing costs.**

⬛ **Best Roth IRA Investments for Maximum Growth:**

- **S&P 500 ETFs (SPY, VOO, IVV)** → 8-10% average annual return.
- **Growth Stocks (AAPL, MSFT, NVDA, TSLA)** → High potential over decades.
- **REITs (Real Estate Investment Trusts)** → Own real estate inside a tax-free Roth.
- **Dividend Growth Stocks (JNJ, KO, PG)** → Passive income + appreciation.

📌 **Example:**

- You borrow **$7,000 at 4% interest** and invest it in a **high-dividend ETF paying 5%**.
- Your **dividends cover the interest**, and the rest **grows tax-free**.

💡 **Lesson:** The tax-free nature of a Roth IRA means you should **prioritize high-growth, high-return investments**.

Step 3: Pay Off the Loan with Roth IRA Gains

Once your Roth IRA grows, you can use **dividends or capital appreciation** to cover the loan repayment.

📌 **Example:**

- Your Roth IRA investments grow **20% in 3 years**.
- You take a **$7,000 withdrawal of contributions** (not earnings—so no penalty!).
- You use that money to **pay off the loan.**

💡 **Result?** Your Roth IRA balance **keeps growing tax-free**, and you've **eliminated the debt**.

Step 4: Use the "Roth Ladder" to Access Money Early

If you plan on retiring before age 59½, you can use the **Roth IRA Ladder strategy** to **withdraw money tax-free**.

How It Works:

- Roth IRA contributions can be **withdrawn anytime tax- and penalty-free**.
- Roth IRA conversions (from Traditional IRAs) **can be withdrawn after 5 years** tax-free.

📌 **Example:**
1. You **convert $10,000 per year from a Traditional IRA to a Roth IRA.**
2. After 5 years, you **withdraw that money tax-free.**
3. Repeat this process every year for an **early retirement income stream.**

💡 **Lesson:** A Roth IRA isn't just for retirement—it can fund **financial independence much earlier.**

Step 5: Keep Repeating This Every Year

This strategy works best if you **fund your Roth IRA consistently, even when cash is tight.**

📌 How to Make It an Annual Habit:
- **Set up automatic Roth IRA contributions** ($583/month = $7,000/year).
- **Use smart borrowing when needed** (HELOC, SBLOC, 0% credit card).
- **Invest aggressively in tax-free growth stocks & ETFs.**
- **Withdraw contributions when needed to pay off short-term debt.**

💡 Result? You never miss a year of tax-free compounding, and **your retirement savings grow exponentially.**

💡 The Takeaway?

Don't let a temporary cash shortage stop you from **maxing out your Roth IRA every year.**

Borrow strategically, invest wisely, and let tax-free compounding work for you.

The next chapter will show you **how to shield your wealth from future tax hikes—so you can keep even more of your money.**

14

Shielding Your Wealth

Avoid Future Tax Hikes with a Backdoor Roth IRA

The Hidden Tax Trap That Could Cost You Millions

If there's one thing we can all agree on, it's this: **Taxes are going up.**

The U.S. national debt is climbing. Social Security is underfunded. Politicians are looking for new ways to raise revenue.

And guess where they'll look first? **Your retirement accounts.**

Most people assume that **tax rates in retirement will be lower**, but that's **a dangerous assumption**.

What if tax rates **increase dramatically** by the time you retire?

What if your **Traditional IRA or 401(k) withdrawals get taxed at 30%, 40%, or even 50%?**

The wealthy have already figured this out—and they're using a **Backdoor Roth IRA** to shield their wealth from future tax hikes.

Now, it's your turn to do the same.

What Is a Backdoor Roth IRA? (And Why Should You Care?)

A **Backdoor Roth IRA** is a legal loophole that allows **high-income earners** to contribute to a **Roth IRA—even if they make too much money.**

Why Would You Want a Roth IRA Instead of a Traditional IRA?

- **Traditional IRA:** You get a tax deduction today, but you'll **pay taxes later** on withdrawals.
- **Roth IRA:** You pay taxes today, but your money **grows and withdraws tax-free—forever.**

📌 **Example:**
If you invest **$1 million in a Roth IRA**, you can withdraw every dollar **tax-free** in retirement—no matter how high tax rates get.

That's why **the rich LOVE Roth IRAs**—they provide a **100% tax-free retirement.**

Who Needs a Backdoor Roth IRA?

Normally, **high earners can't contribute** to a Roth IRA.

📌 **Roth IRA Income Limits for 2024:**

- **Single:** Cannot contribute if you make **$161,000+ per year.**
- **Married (joint filers):** Cannot contribute if you make **$240,000+ per year.**

But there's a **loophole**:

💡 Anyone can convert a Traditional IRA into a Roth IRA—regardless of income.

That's the **Backdoor Roth IRA strategy**—and it's completely legal.

How to Execute a Backdoor Roth IRA (Step-by-Step Guide)

Step 1: Open a Traditional IRA (No Income Limits)

- Choose a brokerage like **Vanguard, Fidelity, or Charles Schwab.**
- **Fund it with after-tax dollars** (since you earn too much for tax-deductible contributions).
- Keep the money in **cash temporarily**—don't invest yet.

Step 2: Immediately Convert the Traditional IRA to a Roth IRA

- Move the funds from your Traditional IRA to your Roth IRA.
- Since you **already paid taxes on your contribution**, there's no extra tax hit.
- Complete this conversion **ASAP** to avoid any taxable gains in the Traditional IRA.

📌 **Pro Tip:** Convert the full amount **within a few days** to avoid any taxable earnings.

Step 3: Invest the Money for Maximum Tax-Free Growth

Now that your money is inside a **Roth IRA**, invest in **high-growth assets** to take full advantage of tax-free compounding.

🔲 **Best Investments for a Backdoor Roth IRA:**

- **S&P 500 ETFs (SPY, VOO, IVV)** → 8-10% annual returns.
- **Growth Stocks (AAPL, TSLA, NVDA, MSFT)** → Maximize long-term growth.
- **Dividend Growth Stocks (JNJ, KO, PG)** → Earn passive income tax-free.
- **REITs (Real Estate Investment Trusts)** → Own real estate without the taxes.

💡 **Lesson:** Since a Roth IRA **grows tax-free**, invest aggressively to **maximize gains.**

Step 4: Repeat Every Year

The IRS allows you to **convert as much as you want** to a Roth IRA—there are no annual limits on conversions.

📌 **Why This Matters:**

- You can **keep executing the Backdoor Roth strategy every year.**
- If tax laws change, you've already locked in tax-free growth for life.

💡 **Pro Tip:** Do this **every single year** to build a massive tax-free retirement account.

The Mega Backdoor Roth IRA (For 401(k) Holders)

If you have access to a **401(k) plan that allows after-tax contributions**, you can take this strategy **even further**.

How It Works:

1. **Max out your 401(k) after-tax contributions** (limit: $46,000 per year in 2024).
2. **Convert those after-tax contributions to a Roth IRA or Roth 401(k).**
3. **Enjoy tax-free growth on an even bigger balance.**

📌 **Example:**
Instead of just putting **$7,000 per year into a Backdoor Roth IRA**, you could convert **$46,000 per year tax-free** through a **Mega Backdoor Roth**.

💡 **Lesson:** If your company allows it, the **Mega Backdoor Roth is the fastest way to build a tax-free fortune.**

Why This Shields Your Wealth from Future Tax Hikes

By converting to a Roth IRA now, you're **locking in today's tax rates**—which are likely much lower than they will be in the future.

📌 **Historical Tax Rate Trends:**

Year	Top Tax Bracket
1981	70%
2000	39.6%
2024	37%
2030?	??? (Probably Higher)

💡 **The Risk:** If you leave your money in a **Traditional IRA**, you might be forced to pay **much higher taxes on withdrawals in retirement.**

📌 **Example:**

- If you have **$2 million in a Traditional IRA**, and tax rates rise to **50%**, you'll owe **$1 million in taxes** over time.
- But if you converted to a **Roth IRA today**, your withdrawals would be **100% tax-free forever.**

💡 **Lesson: Taxes are on sale today.** Converting now saves you from paying much higher rates later.

Common Myths About the Backdoor Roth IRA

✗ **"Isn't this illegal?"** → No, it's completely legal. The IRS has acknowledged the Backdoor Roth strategy.

✗ **"Won't the government close this loophole?"** → Maybe, but if you convert now, **they can't take away your tax-free gains.**

✗ **"I make too much to qualify for a Roth IRA."** → That's exactly why the Backdoor Roth IRA exists.

✗ **"I don't want to pay taxes now."** → You'll pay far more in the future if tax rates rise.

💡 **The Takeaway?**

Future tax hikes are coming. **Don't wait until retirement to find out how much you'll owe.**

Convert to a Roth IRA **now** and shield your wealth from the IRS **forever.**

The next chapter will show you how to **turn losses into gains—using tax-loss harvesting to legally reduce your tax bill.**

15

SPY vs SPY vs SPY

One ETF, Three Outcomes

When most people invest in the stock market, they assume their returns depend solely on **which stocks they pick** or **how the market performs.**

But what if I told you that **the same exact investment—SPY, the most popular S&P 500 ETF—could result in completely different financial outcomes** based on how you manage it?

That's right.

You and your neighbor could both invest **$100,000 into SPY**, but one of you might retire with **$500,000 tax-free**, while the other ends up with **half that amount after taxes**—all because of the choices you make.

In this chapter, we'll break down the **three different paths you can take with the same SPY investment—and which one will make you the most money.**

What Is SPY? (And Why Does It Matter?)

📌 **SPY (SPDR S&P 500 ETF)** is the largest and most actively traded **exchange-traded fund (ETF)** that tracks the **S&P 500 Index.**

Why Investors Love SPY:

■ **Diversification** → Holds 500 of the biggest U.S. companies.
■ **8-10% average annual return** → Strong historical performance.
■ **Liquidity** → Easy to buy and sell.

💡 **The Key Question:** If SPY is the same for everyone, why do some investors **end up with more money** than others?

Let's look at three different ways you could handle an SPY investment—and how they impact your wealth.

Scenario #1: Buy SPY in a Taxable Account and Sell in Retirement

This is the most **common** approach investors take.

📌 **How It Works:**

- You buy **$100,000 of SPY** in a **regular brokerage account** (not a retirement account).
- You let it grow for **30 years** at an average **8% return.**
- Your balance grows to **$1,000,000** by retirement.
- You sell shares to fund your retirement.

📌 **The Problem? Taxes.**

- Every time you sell shares, you pay **capital gains tax**.
- If tax rates increase, you could owe **30%+ in taxes** on withdrawals.
- If you pass it down to heirs, they get a **stepped-up cost basis**, but you never benefited from tax-free compounding.

💡 Outcome: $1,000,000 sounds great—but you'll owe massive taxes when you withdraw.

Scenario #2: Buy SPY in a Traditional IRA and Withdraw in Retirement

This is how many **retirement-focused** investors handle their SPY investments.

📌 **How It Works:**

- You buy **$100,000 of SPY** inside a **Traditional IRA** (pre-tax money).
- It grows **tax-deferred** to **$1,000,000** over 30 years.
- You withdraw money in retirement.

📌 **The Problem? Required Minimum Distributions (RMDs) & Taxes.**

- At age 73, the IRS **forces you to take withdrawals (RMDs).**
- Every withdrawal is taxed as **ordinary income** (not capital gains).
- If tax rates increase, you could lose **40%+ of your withdrawals to taxes.**

💡 Outcome: You delayed taxes, but you'll still owe them later—at possibly higher rates.

Scenario #3: Buy SPY in a Roth IRA and Withdraw Tax-Free

This is the **ultimate wealth-building strategy** for SPY investors.

📌 How It Works:

- You buy **$100,000 of SPY** inside a **Roth IRA** (after-tax money).
- It grows **tax-free** to **$1,000,000** over 30 years.
- You withdraw money in retirement **100% tax-free**.

📌 Why This Is the Best Strategy:
⬛ No capital gains taxes.
⬛ No RMDs—your money grows tax-free forever.
⬛ You can pass it to heirs tax-free.

💡 Outcome: You keep all $1,000,000 tax-free—no IRS cut.

Side-by-Side Comparison: Which SPY Strategy Wins?

Scenario	Initial Investment	Growth (30 Years at 8%)	Taxes	Final Amount
SPY in Taxable Account	$100,000	$1,000,000	Capital gains tax (15-30%)	~$700,000
SPY in Traditional IRA	$100,000	$1,000,000	Income tax (25-40%)	~$600,000
SPY in Roth IRA	$100,000	$1,000,000	$0 (Tax-Free)	$1,000,000

💡 **Winner: Roth IRA** → You keep every penny of your investment **tax-free**.

How to Use SPY to Create Tax-Free Wealth

Step 1: Max Out a Roth IRA Every Year

- Contribution limit: **$7,000/year ($8,000 if 50+)**.
- If you make too much, use a **Backdoor Roth IRA**.

Step 2: Invest Your Roth IRA in SPY (or Other S&P 500 ETFs)

- **SPY, VOO, or IVV** → All track the S&P 500.
- Avoid holding bonds—**your Roth IRA should focus on growth.**

Step 3: Never Sell—Let It Compound Tax-Free

- The longer you hold SPY, the **more you benefit from tax-free growth.**
- If you need cash before retirement, use a **Roth Ladder to withdraw penalty-free.**

Step 4: Use a Roth IRA for Generational Wealth

- Roth IRAs have **no Required Minimum Distributions (RMDs).**
- If you pass it to your kids, they **inherit tax-free wealth.**

📌 **Example:**
If your Roth IRA grows to **$5 million**, your heirs can **inherit all $5 million tax-free.**

💡 **Lesson: SPY in a Roth IRA is the closest thing to free money you'll ever find.**

16

Municipal Bonds

"Munis" for Tax-Free Money

For most investors, the biggest enemy isn't market crashes—it's **taxes**.

The more money you make, the **more the IRS takes**.

- **Capital gains taxes eat into your stock profits.**
- **Ordinary income taxes take a chunk of your paycheck.**
- **Even Social Security benefits can get taxed if you earn too much in retirement.**

But what if there was a way to **earn investment income completely tax-free**?

There is.

They're called **municipal bonds (a.k.a. "Munis")**, and they are one of the **best-kept secrets** for tax-free income.

What Are Municipal Bonds?

Municipal bonds (Munis) are **loans you give to state and local governments**.

In return, the government pays you **tax-free interest.**

Why Investors Love Munis:

- **No Federal Taxes** → Munis are exempt from federal income tax.
- **State Tax-Free (In Your State)** → If you buy bonds from your own state, you don't pay state taxes either.
- **Steady, Predictable Income** → Unlike stocks, muni bonds pay a **fixed interest rate**.

💡 Think of Munis as a tax-free paycheck that pays you every month.

How "Munis" Create Tax-Free Wealth

📌 **Example: A $1 Million Municipal Bond Portfolio**

- You invest **$1,000,000 in municipal bonds** paying a **5% interest rate**.
- That's **$50,000 per year in income—100% tax-free**.
- If you were in the **35% tax bracket**, you'd need to earn **$76,923 from a taxable investment** just to match the same $50,000 after taxes.

💡 **Lesson:** The higher your tax bracket, the more valuable Munis become.

Who Should Invest in Municipal Bonds?

Munis are perfect for investors who:
■ Want **stable, passive income.**
■ Are in a **high tax bracket** (Munis provide the most value to top earners).
■ Need **low-risk investments** for retirement.

📌 **Who Benefits the Most from Munis?**

- **Doctors, Lawyers, and High-Income Earners** → Avoid high federal & state taxes.
- **Retirees** → Get steady, tax-free income.
- **Early Retirees** → Use Munis to **reduce taxable income** while still generating cash flow.

The Two Types of Municipal Bonds (Which One Should You Buy?)

There are two main types of Munis:

Type	What It Funds	Risk Level	Best For
General Obligation Bonds (GO Bonds)	Roads, schools, infrastructure	Lower risk	Conservative investors
Revenue Bonds	Fund toll roads, airports, hospitals (backed by revenue)	Slightly higher risk	Investors seeking higher yields

📌 Which One Is Better?

- If you want maximum safety → Go for **General Obligation Bonds (GO Bonds)**.
- If you want higher returns → Consider **Revenue Bonds** with strong revenue streams.

How to Invest in Municipal Bonds

There are **three ways to buy Munis**:

Option #1: Buy Individual Municipal Bonds

- You purchase specific bonds from your **state or city**.
- Hold them until **maturity** to get your full investment back.

💡 Best for: Investors who want **full control** over their bonds.

📌 Example: Buying a **California Muni Bond** means **no federal or state tax** for California residents.

Option #2: Buy a Municipal Bond Fund (ETF or Mutual Fund)

- **Easier than buying individual bonds.**
- Provides **instant diversification** across multiple states and cities.
- Some of the most popular **Muni ETFs:**
    - **VTEB (Vanguard Tax-Exempt Bond ETF)**
    - **MUB (iShares National Muni Bond ETF)**
    - **TFTAX (Tax-Free Bond Mutual Fund from Fidelity)**

💡 Best for: Investors who want **passive exposure to Munis** without picking individual bonds.

Option #3: Buy High-Yield Municipal Bonds for Bigger Returns

- These bonds **pay higher interest** but come with **more risk**.
- Often used for projects like **hospitals, stadiums, and new developments**.
- Look for bonds with **high credit ratings (AA or AAA)**.

💡 Best for: Investors willing to take on **slightly more risk** for **higher returns**.

How Municipal Bonds Fit Into a Buy, Borrow, Die Strategy

We already know that **the wealthy don't sell their assets—they borrow against them.**

Here's how they use **municipal bonds to create tax-free wealth:**

📌 **Example: The $10 Million Tax-Free Borrowing Strategy**
1. A wealthy investor buys **$10 million worth of municipal bonds** paying 5% interest.
2. That's **$500,000 per year in tax-free income.**
3. Instead of selling bonds, they **borrow against them at 3% interest.**
4. They now have **$500,000 of tax-free income AND access to borrowed money.**

💡 **Lesson:** The rich don't just **collect tax-free income**—they also **borrow against it to avoid ever paying taxes.**

Are Municipal Bonds Right for You? (Pros & Cons)

■ Pros of Municipal Bonds:

✔ **Tax-free income** (especially valuable for high earners).
✔ **Lower risk** than stocks.
✔ **Reliable cash flow** for retirees.
✔ **Easy to hold inside tax-advantaged accounts** (IRAs, brokerage accounts).

✖ Cons of Municipal Bonds:

✖ **Lower returns than stocks** over long periods.
✖ **Inflation can eat away at bond income.**
✖ **Some bonds have default risk** (always check credit ratings).

💡 **The Solution?** Don't go all-in on bonds—use them **alongside stocks & real estate** for a balanced portfolio.

17

Minimizing Your Tax Bill

Strategies for Reducing Capital Gains Taxes

Every time you sell an investment for a profit, the IRS takes a cut.

That's called **capital gains tax**, and if you're not careful, it can eat away at **thousands (or even millions) of dollars of your wealth** over time.

But here's what the rich understand that most people don't:

You don't have to pay capital gains taxes—at least not right away.

With the right strategies, you can **delay, reduce, or even eliminate** capital gains taxes entirely.

In this chapter, we'll cover the most **powerful tax-saving strategies** that the wealthy use—so you can keep more of your investment profits instead of handing them over to the IRS.

What Are Capital Gains Taxes (And Why Do They Matter)?

📌 **A capital gain happens when you sell an asset for more than you paid for it.**

- If you **bought a stock for $10,000 and sold it for $20,000**, you have a **$10,000 capital gain**—which is **taxable**.

📌 **Capital Gains Tax Rates (2024):**

Filing Status	0% Tax Rate (Income Below)	15% Tax Rate	20% Tax Rate (Income Above)
Single	$44,625	$44,626 - $492,300	$492,301+
Married (Joint)	$89,250	$89,251 - $553,850	$553,851+

💡 **Lesson:** If you're in a high-income bracket, you could be paying **20%+ in capital gains taxes** every time you sell an investment.

That's why the rich use **loopholes to reduce or eliminate these taxes.**

Strategy #1: Hold Investments for at Least One Year (Avoid Short-Term Gains Taxes)

Not all capital gains are taxed the same.

📌 **Short-Term Capital Gains (Held Less Than 1 Year)**

- Taxed at **ordinary income rates** (up to 37%).

📌 **Long-Term Capital Gains (Held More Than 1 Year)**

- Taxed at **lower rates (0%, 15%, or 20%).**

💡 **Example:**

- If you buy a stock and sell it **after 6 months**, you'll pay **income tax rates (up to 37%).**
- If you wait **12+ months**, your tax rate **drops to 15% or 20%.**

💡 **Lesson:** Always hold investments for **at least a year** to take advantage of **lower tax rates.**

Strategy #2: Use Tax-Loss Harvesting (Turn Losses into Tax Savings)

Sometimes, your investments lose money. But instead of seeing losses as a setback, **the wealthy use them to reduce their tax bill.**

This is called **tax-loss harvesting**—and it can save you thousands.

How It Works:

1. **Sell an investment at a loss** to generate a **capital loss.**
2. **Use that loss to offset capital gains.**
3. If you have more losses than gains, you can deduct up to $3,000 from your regular income.
4. **Reinvest in a similar asset** (to keep your portfolio on track).

📌 **Example:**

- You sell **Stock A** at a **$10,000 loss**.
- You sell **Stock B** at a **$10,000 gain**.
- Normally, you'd owe **capital gains taxes on Stock B**—but because of the **Stock A loss, you pay $0 in taxes.**

💡 **Lesson:** The rich **never waste a loss**—they turn it into a tax advantage.

Strategy #3: Borrow Against Assets Instead of Selling (The Buy, Borrow, Die Strategy)

The best way to avoid capital gains tax? **Never sell your investments.**

Instead of selling, the wealthy **borrow against their assets** to get tax-free cash.

📌 **How It Works:**
1. Build a portfolio of **stocks, real estate, or other assets**.
2. Instead of selling, take out a **securities-based line of credit (SBLOC)** or a **home equity loan (HELOC)**.
3. Use the borrowed money **to fund your lifestyle, buy more investments, or reinvest.**

💡 **Example:**

- You have **$1 million in stocks**.
- Instead of selling (and triggering taxes), you **borrow $500,000 at 4% interest**.
- Your investments keep growing, and you never pay capital gains tax.

💡 **Lesson:** Borrowing against assets lets you **access wealth without ever triggering taxes.**

Strategy #4: Invest Through a Roth IRA (Completely Eliminate Capital Gains Taxes)

A **Roth IRA** is the **best tax-free investment account** available.

📌 **Why?**

- You **pay taxes upfront** on contributions.
- Your investments **grow tax-free**.
- You can withdraw **100% tax-free in retirement**.

💡 **Example:**

- You invest **$10,000 in SPY (S&P 500 ETF)** inside a Roth IRA.
- Over 30 years, it grows to **$150,000**.
- When you withdraw, you **pay $0 in capital gains taxes.**

💡 **Lesson:** A Roth IRA is **the easiest way** to permanently avoid capital gains tax.

Strategy #5: Use the 1031 Exchange to Defer Real Estate Taxes

If you invest in **real estate**, you can use a **1031 exchange** to **defer capital gains taxes forever.**

How It Works:

1. Sell an investment property.
2. Use the proceeds to **buy a new property** of equal or greater value.
3. Pay **$0 in capital gains tax**—the taxes roll over to the new property.
4. Keep doing this until **you pass the real estate to your heirs (who get a stepped-up cost basis and pay $0 in taxes).**

📌 **Example:**

- You buy a rental property for **$500,000** and sell it for **$1 million**.
- Normally, you'd owe **capital gains tax on $500,000**.
- Instead, you **use a 1031 exchange to buy another property** and pay **$0 in taxes.**

💡 **Lesson:** The rich **never sell real estate outright—they exchange it and defer taxes indefinitely.**

18

Turning Losses into Gains

How Tax-Loss Harvesting Can Save You Money

Most people see investment losses as a **bad thing**.

But the wealthy? They see losses as **an opportunity to pay less in taxes** and grow their wealth even faster.

This strategy is called **tax-loss harvesting**, and it's one of the most powerful ways to turn **market downturns into tax savings**—while keeping your portfolio on track.

In this chapter, I'll show you exactly how to use tax-loss harvesting to **reduce your tax bill, boost your investment returns, and keep more of your money.**

What Is Tax-Loss Harvesting (And Why Does It Matter)?

Tax-loss harvesting is a strategy that allows you to **sell losing investments, use those losses to offset taxable gains, and reinvest in similar assets—so your portfolio stays intact.**

📌 How It Works:
1. **Sell an investment at a loss** to generate a tax deduction.
2. **Use that loss to offset capital gains** (reducing the taxes you owe).
3. **Reinvest the money into a similar asset** so you stay invested.

💡 Result? You **reduce your tax bill without actually reducing your investment exposure.**

Why Tax-Loss Harvesting Is a Game-Changer

Most investors only think about **gains**, but what they don't realize is that **losses can be just as valuable—if used correctly.**

The Three Ways You Benefit from Tax-Loss Harvesting:

■ **1. Reduce Capital Gains Taxes** → Use losses to offset gains from profitable investments.
■ **2. Lower Your Ordinary Income Tax Bill** → Deduct up to **$3,000 per year** from your regular income.
■ **3. Carry Forward Excess Losses** → If your losses exceed your gains, you can **roll them forward to future years.**

📌 **Example: How a $10,000 Loss Saves You Money**

- You sell **Stock A** and realize a **$10,000 loss**.
- You sell **Stock B** with a **$10,000 gain**.
- Normally, you'd owe **15-20% capital gains tax on Stock B**—but thanks to the Stock A loss, you owe **$0 in taxes.**

💡 **Lesson:** If you're going to take a loss, **make it work for you.**

Step-by-Step Guide to Tax-Loss Harvesting

Step 1: Identify Losing Investments

Look at your **portfolio** for stocks, ETFs, or other assets that are **trading below your purchase price.**

📌 **Best Time to Harvest Losses:**

- **Market downturns** (big crashes provide more tax-saving opportunities).
- **End of the year** (so you can reduce your tax bill before filing).

💡 **Pro Tip:** Don't wait until December—**harvest losses throughout the year when opportunities arise.**

Step 2: Sell the Losing Investment

Once you identify a **losing stock, ETF, or crypto asset**, you sell it to **realize the loss.**

📌 **Important Rule:** Losses are only **realized** when you sell—paper losses don't count.

💡 **Example:**

- You bought **Amazon stock at $3,500 per share**.
- It drops to **$2,500 per share**—a **$1,000 loss per share**.
- You sell to **realize the loss** and use it for tax benefits.

Step 3: Reinvest the Money in a Similar Asset (Avoid the Wash-Sale Rule)

The biggest mistake investors make with tax-loss harvesting is **buying back the same stock too soon**.

📌 **The Wash-Sale Rule:**

- You **can't buy the same stock (or a substantially identical security)** within **30 days before or after** selling at a loss.
- If you do, the **IRS won't let you use the loss for tax deductions**.

💡 **Solution:** Instead of buying back the same stock, **buy a similar asset** to keep your portfolio balanced.

📌 **Example: How to Avoid the Wash-Sale Rule**

Sold Investment	Replacement Investment
Sold **SPY (S&P 500 ETF)**	Buy **VOO (Vanguard S&P 500 ETF)**
Sold **Apple (AAPL)**	Buy **Microsoft (MSFT)**
Sold **Tesla (TSLA)**	Buy **General Motors (GM)**

💡 **Lesson:** This way, you **stay invested in the market** while still locking in **tax savings**.

Step 4: Use the Loss to Offset Gains & Income

Once you realize the loss, it can be used in **three ways:**

1️⃣ **Offset Capital Gains** → If you have a $10,000 loss and a $10,000 gain, your taxable gain is **$0**.
2️⃣ **Offset Ordinary Income** → If you have more losses than gains, you can **deduct up to $3,000 per year** against your income.
3️⃣ **Carry Forward Excess Losses** → If your losses exceed $3,000, the extra amount **rolls over to future years**.

📌 **Example: How to Stack Tax Savings Over Multiple Years**

- Year 1: You take a **$50,000 loss.**
- You offset **$10,000 in capital gains** → **$40,000 loss remaining.**
- You deduct **$3,000 from your ordinary income** → **$37,000 loss remaining.**
- The remaining **$37,000 loss rolls over to next year** (and keeps reducing taxes).

💡 **Lesson:** One big loss can **reduce your tax bill for years.**

Advanced Strategies: How the Wealthy Take Tax-Loss Harvesting Even Further

1. Tax-Loss Harvesting with Crypto (No Wash-Sale Rule!)

Unlike stocks, crypto is **not subject to the wash-sale rule.**

📌 **What This Means:**

- You can **sell Bitcoin at a loss** and **immediately buy it back**—while still getting the tax benefit.
- This makes **crypto the ultimate tax-loss harvesting tool.**

💡 **Pro Tip:** If you're holding crypto at a loss, **consider harvesting losses before this loophole closes.**

2. Use Tax-Loss Harvesting for Early Retirement (Roth Conversion Strategy)

If you plan to retire early, you can use tax-loss harvesting to **offset the taxes on Roth IRA conversions.**

📌 **How It Works:**

- Convert **Traditional IRA funds to a Roth IRA** (this triggers taxes).
- Use **harvested tax losses to offset the tax bill** from the conversion.
- Result? **You pay little or no taxes on your Roth conversion.**

💡 **Lesson:** This is how early retirees move money **from taxable accounts into tax-free Roth IRAs—without paying heavy taxes.**

19

Borrow, Again

If You Can't Beat 'Em, Join 'Em

For years, we've been told that **debt is bad.**

✗ **Avoid loans.**
✗ **Pay off your mortgage early.**
✗ **Never borrow money unless you have to.**

But if that were true, why do the **wealthiest people in the world borrow more money than anyone else?**

The answer is simple:

💡 **The rich don't use debt to buy liabilities**—they use it to build tax-free wealth.

In this chapter, we'll break down why borrowing is **one of the most powerful wealth-building tools** and how you can use it to grow your money **just like the ultra-rich.**

Why Borrowing Is the Secret to Unlimited Wealth

If you've been following along, you already know the golden rule of the **Buy, Borrow, Die** strategy:

📌 **Never sell your assets. Borrow against them instead.**

This allows you to:
■ **Avoid capital gains taxes** (because loans aren't taxable).
■ **Let your investments keep compounding** (instead of selling).
■ **Pass down assets tax-free to your heirs** (with a stepped-up cost basis).

💡 **Lesson:** The rich don't work for money—they borrow money against their assets and let their wealth grow tax-free.

Now let's look at the **best ways to borrow like the wealthy.**

The Three Best Ways to Borrow Against Your Assets

Not all debt is bad. **There's good debt and bad debt.**

📌 **Bad debt** = Credit cards, personal loans, car loans.
📌 **Good debt** = Borrowing against appreciating assets to invest in more assets.

Here are the three best ways to **borrow tax-free and build wealth.**

1. Borrow Against Stocks (Securities-Based Line of Credit - SBLOC)

If you have a stock portfolio, you can take out a **securities-based line of credit (SBLOC)** instead of selling your stocks.

📌 **How It Works:**

- You own **$500,000 in stocks**.
- Instead of selling (and triggering taxes), you **borrow $250,000 at 3-5% interest**.
- You use that money **to invest in real estate, buy more stocks, or fund your lifestyle**.

📌 **Why It's Powerful:**
■ You don't sell your stocks, so they keep growing.
■ The loan interest is often tax-deductible.
■ You can borrow up to 70% of your portfolio's value.

💡 **Lesson:** Borrowing against stocks gives you **cash without ever paying capital gains taxes.**

2. Borrow Against Your Home (HELOC & Cash-Out Refinance)

Instead of paying off your house early, **use home equity to create wealth.**

📌 **Two Ways to Borrow from Your Home:**
1️⃣ **Home Equity Line of Credit (HELOC)** → A flexible credit line using your home as collateral.
2️⃣ **Cash-Out Refinance** → Replaces your mortgage with a new, bigger loan—and you keep the difference in cash.

📌 **Example: Using a HELOC to Buy More Assets**

- Your home is worth **$500,000**, and you have **$250,000 in equity**.

- You take out a **$150,000 HELOC at 5% interest**.
- You use the money to **buy rental properties or invest in stocks paying 10% returns**.
- Your assets grow **faster than your loan interest**, making you more money over time.

💡 **Lesson:** Instead of letting your home equity sit idle, **put it to work**.

3. Borrow Against Whole Life Insurance (Policy Loans)

Most people don't realize that **you can take tax-free loans from your life insurance policy**.

📌 **How It Works:**

- You buy a **Whole Life or Indexed Universal Life (IUL) insurance policy**.
- The policy builds up **cash value** over time.
- You **borrow against the cash value** tax-free—without ever paying back the loan (it's deducted from your death benefit).

📌 **Why It's Powerful:**
■ **Loans are tax-free.**
■ **No credit checks or repayment schedules.**
■ **Your policy keeps growing even while you borrow against it.**

💡 **Lesson:** The rich use life insurance as a **personal bank**—accessing tax-free cash while still building wealth.

How the Ultra-Wealthy Use Debt to Multiply Their Wealth

If you want to **think like the rich**, you need to understand **how they use borrowing to grow their fortunes**.

📌 **Example: The $10 Million Borrowing Strategy**

- A billionaire has **$100 million in stocks**.
- Instead of selling, he **borrows $10 million at 3% interest**.
- He reinvests that money in **real estate earning 8% returns**.
- He makes **$800,000 per year from the real estate**, while his stocks **keep growing**.

💡 **Lesson:** The rich **don't use their own money—they use cheap debt to make more money.**

How to Borrow Like the Wealthy (Without Going Broke)

Borrowing is powerful—but only **if you use it correctly.**

■ The Right Way to Borrow:

✔ **Only borrow against assets that appreciate** (stocks, real estate, businesses).
✔ **Use debt to buy more income-generating assets.**
✔ **Make sure your investment returns are higher than your borrowing costs.**

📌 **Example: Borrowing Smart vs. Borrowing Stupid**

Smart Borrowing	Bad Borrowing
Taking a **3% loan** to buy real estate earning 10% returns.	Taking a **7% personal loan** to buy a **new car**.
Using a **HELOC** to invest in **rental properties**.	Using a HELOC to **remodel your kitchen** with no financial return.
Borrowing against **stocks** to buy more stocks.	Borrowing against **stocks** to go on vacation.

💡 **Lesson: Use debt to buy assets—not liabilities.**

The Biggest Myth: "I Want to Be Debt-Free"

Many people say their goal is to **be debt-free**—but that's a mistake.

The real goal isn't to **avoid debt**—it's to **use debt wisely.**

📌 **Consider This:**

- A **debt-free** person with $500,000 in the bank earns **1-2% interest.**
- A wealthy investor borrows **$500,000 at 4% interest** and reinvests it in **assets earning 10%.**
- The investor makes **$30,000+ per year** while the debt-free person stays stuck.

💡 **Lesson: The wealthy leverage debt to build wealth faster.**

PART TWO

Real Estate

The second Pillar of a Buy, Borrow, Die strategy

20

Unlocking Tax-Free Savings

The 2024 First-Time Homebuyers Tax Credit

For most people, buying a home is the **biggest financial decision they'll ever make**—but it's also one of the best ways to build wealth.

And now, with the **2024 First-Time Homebuyers Tax Credit**, the government is making it **easier and more affordable than ever** to purchase your first home.

This chapter will break down **how the tax credit works, who qualifies, and how to maximize your savings**—so you can turn homeownership into a **tax-free wealth-building machine**.

What Is the 2024 First-Time Homebuyers Tax Credit?

The **First-Time Homebuyers Tax Credit** is a **federal incentive program** that helps first-time buyers **save money on their home purchase.**

📌 **Key Benefits:**
■ **Up to $15,000 tax credit** for first-time buyers.
■ **Direct reduction of your tax bill** (not just a deduction).
■ **Doesn't have to be repaid** (unlike the old 2008 version).
■ **Can be combined with other homebuyer programs.**

💡 **Why This Matters:** If you qualify, the tax credit **directly reduces what you owe the IRS**—which could mean **thousands of dollars in savings.**

Who Qualifies for the 2024 First-Time Homebuyers Tax Credit?

To qualify for this tax credit, you must meet these requirements:

📌 **1. You Must Be a First-Time Homebuyer**

- A **first-time homebuyer** is someone who hasn't owned a home in the past **3 years**.
- If you're buying with a spouse, **both of you must be first-time buyers** to qualify.

📌 **2. You Must Meet the Income Limits**

- The credit is **phased out for high earners**—exact limits vary by location.
- Generally, you must earn **below 150% of the area's median income** to qualify.

📌 **3. The Home Must Be Your Primary Residence**

- You must live in the home as **your main residence** for at least **4 years**.
- If you sell before then, **you may have to repay part of the credit.**

📌 **4. You Must Buy a Qualifying Home**

- Single-family homes, condos, townhouses, and some co-ops qualify.
- **Investment properties and vacation homes DO NOT qualify.**

💡 **Lesson:** If you meet these requirements, you could get **up to $15,000 in free tax savings** just for buying a home.

How Much Can You Actually Save?

📌 **Example 1: A Homebuyer Saving $10,000 on Taxes**

- Sarah buys her first home for **$350,000**.
- She qualifies for the **full $10,000 tax credit**.
- Normally, she owes **$12,000 in federal taxes**.
- After applying the tax credit, she now only owes **$2,000**.

📌 **Example 2: A Homebuyer Gets a $15,000 Refund**

- James buys a home for **$400,000**.
- He qualifies for the **full $15,000 tax credit**.

- He only owed **$8,000 in taxes**, so after applying the credit, he gets a **$7,000 tax refund!**

💡 **Lesson:** This tax credit isn't just a deduction—it's **real cash in your pocket.**

How to Claim the First-Time Homebuyer Tax Credit

🟥 **Step 1: Check Your Eligibility**

- Review your income, home purchase status, and residency requirements.

🟥 **Step 2: Buy a Qualifying Home**

- Make sure the home is your **primary residence** and meets program guidelines.

🟥 **Step 3: File the Correct Forms with the IRS**

- You'll need to **claim the credit when filing your taxes** for the year you bought the home.
- Work with a **tax professional** to ensure you file correctly.

🟥 **Step 4: Combine with Other Homebuyer Benefits**

- Look into **state & local homebuyer programs** that may offer additional credits or down payment assistance.

💡 **Pro Tip:** Some states **match federal tax credits**—meaning you could get even more savings.

Can You Combine This Credit with Other Homebuyer Programs?

YES! You can **stack multiple homebuyer programs together** to maximize your savings.

📌 **Other First-Time Homebuyer Assistance Programs (2024):**

Program	Benefit	Who Qualifies?
FHA Loan	3.5% down payment	Credit score 580+
VA Loan	0% down payment	Military service members
USDA Loan	0% down in rural areas	Must meet income limits
State Homebuyer Grants	Up to $25,000	Varies by state
Down Payment Assistance Programs	Low-interest or forgivable loans	First-time buyers

📍 **Lesson:** If you qualify, you could **combine multiple programs** to buy a home with **little to no out-of-pocket costs.**

How This Fits Into the Buy, Borrow, Die Strategy

Buying a home isn't just about having a place to live—it's about **building long-term, tax-free wealth.**

Here's how:

📌 **Step 1: Buy a Home with Tax-Free Savings**

- Use the **First-Time Homebuyer Tax Credit** to **reduce your upfront costs.**

📌 **Step 2: Build Equity Over Time**

- As your home appreciates, you gain **equity** that you can later borrow against.

📌 **Step 3: Borrow Against Your Home Instead of Selling**

- Once your home increases in value, **take out a HELOC or cash-out refinance** to access cash **tax-free**.

📌 **Step 4: Use That Cash to Invest**

- Take the **borrowed money** and invest in **stocks, rental properties, or a business**—all while keeping your home.

📌 **Step 5: Pass It Down Tax-Free**

- Your heirs **inherit the home with a stepped-up cost basis**—meaning they **avoid capital gains taxes.**

📍 **Lesson:** Homeownership isn't just about **where you live—it's a tool to build lasting, generational wealth.**

21

Leveraging OPM

The Tax-Efficient Path to Homeownership

Most people think you need to save for years, build perfect credit, and have a **huge down payment** to buy a home.

But the wealthy? They know the secret:

💡 You don't need your own money to buy a home—you just need access to Other People's Money (OPM).

By using **loans, tax credits, and leverage**, you can buy real estate with **little to no out-of-pocket cost**—while using the **tax code to your advantage**.

In this chapter, I'll show you how to:
- ■ Use OPM to buy a home without depleting your cash.
- ■ Leverage tax breaks to make homeownership even cheaper.
- ■ Turn your home into a tax-free wealth-building machine.

What Is OPM (And Why Should You Use It)?

OPM = Using other people's money to finance your investments.

Most wealthy investors **never use their own money** to buy real estate. Instead, they use:
- 📌 **Bank loans** (mortgages, HELOCs, investment loans).
- 📌 **Government-backed programs** (FHA, VA, USDA loans).
- 📌 **Tax credits and deductions** (to lower costs).
- 📌 **Seller financing** (negotiating directly with sellers).

💡 **Why This Works:** Real estate is an appreciating asset—meaning you can **use debt to buy it, let it increase in value, and keep the profits.**

Step 1: Choose the Right Mortgage (Buy With as Little as 0% Down)

Most people assume they need **20% down** to buy a home. That's a **myth**.

📌 **Government-Backed Loan Options (Low or No Down Payment):**

Loan Type	Down Payment	Best For
FHA Loan	3.5%	First-time homebuyers with 580+ credit score
VA Loan	0%	Military veterans & active service members
USDA Loan	0%	Rural & suburban homebuyers
Conventional Loan (First-Time Buyers)	3%	Buyers with good credit (620+)

📌 **Example: Buying a $400,000 Home with OPM**

- Instead of paying **$80,000 (20% down)**...
- You qualify for an **FHA loan and put down just $14,000 (3.5%)**...
- You keep **$66,000 in cash to invest elsewhere.**

💡 **Lesson:** The less cash you put into the house, the more you can use **for investments that grow faster.**

Step 2: Use Tax Credits & Deductions to Reduce Your Costs

The IRS **rewards** homeowners with tax breaks that renters don't get.

📌 **Key Homeowner Tax Benefits:**

Tax Benefit	How Much Can You Save?
Mortgage Interest Deduction	Deducts **interest paid on loan** (up to $750,000 mortgage).
Property Tax Deduction	Deducts up to **$10,000** in property taxes.
Mortgage Insurance Premiums (FHA Loans)	Fully deductible for **low-income buyers.**
First-Time Homebuyer Tax Credit (2024)	Up to **$15,000** for qualifying buyers.
Energy-Efficient Home Tax Credits	**$1,200+ in annual credits** for solar panels, insulation, etc.

📌 **Example: How Tax Breaks Save You Thousands**

- You buy a **$400,000 home** with an **FHA loan**.
- Your **annual mortgage interest = $12,000** → Deductible from taxable income.
- Your **property taxes = $5,000** → Also deductible.
- You claim the **First-Time Homebuyer Tax Credit** → Saves you **$15,000 immediately**.

💡 **Lesson:** Owning a home **lowers your tax bill every year**—giving you more money to invest.

Step 3: Use Seller Financing (Buy a Home with No Bank Involved)

📌 **What Is Seller Financing?**

- Instead of getting a **mortgage from a bank**, you **make payments directly to the seller**.
- No **credit check, bank approval, or large down payment needed**.

📌 **Why This Works:**
■ **Easier approval** (especially if you have bad credit or inconsistent income).
■ **No loan origination fees** (saving you thousands).
■ **Negotiable terms** (lower interest rates, no prepayment penalties).

📌 **Example: How Seller Financing Works**

- A seller owns a home worth **$300,000** but **wants to sell fast**.
- Instead of getting a mortgage, you agree to **pay them $2,000/month for 15 years**.
- After 15 years, you **own the home outright—no bank needed**.

💡 **Lesson:** Seller financing lets you **own a home without going through a bank**—often with **better terms**.

Step 4: House Hack (Live for Free & Build Wealth at the Same Time)

Want to **own a home but not pay a mortgage?** House hacking lets you **live for free while someone else pays your mortgage**.

📌 **House Hacking Strategies:**
■ **Buy a multi-unit property (duplex, triplex, fourplex)** → Rent out the extra units.
■ **Rent out extra rooms on Airbnb.**
■ **Live in one part of the house & rent the rest.**

📌 **Example: House Hacking a Duplex**

- You buy a **$500,000 duplex** with an **FHA loan (3.5% down)**.
- You live in **one unit and rent the other for $2,000/month.**
- Your mortgage payment = **$2,500/month** → The rent covers most of it.
- **You live for nearly free** while your **tenant pays your mortgage.**

💡 **Lesson:** House hacking turns your home into a **cash-flowing investment**—instead of a liability.

Step 5: Borrow Against Your Home (HELOC or Cash-Out Refi) to Invest

Once your home appreciates, **use its value to borrow tax-free.**

📌 **Two Ways to Access Home Equity:**
1️⃣ **HELOC (Home Equity Line of Credit)** → Borrow against your home's equity **like a credit card**.
2️⃣ **Cash-Out Refinance** → Replace your mortgage with a new one, pulling **out the difference in cash**.

📌 **Example: Turning $100K in Home Equity Into $500K in Investments**

- Your home value increases by **$100,000**.
- Instead of selling, you **borrow $80,000 tax-free**.
- You use that money to **buy a rental property generating $2,500/month.**
- Your rental income pays off the loan—and you still own your first home.

💡 **Lesson:** Borrowing against home equity lets you **keep your house while using its value to buy more assets.**

22

The Home Mortgage Deduction

Home Sweet Tax Break

Owning a home isn't just about having a place to live—it's about leveraging one of the biggest **tax breaks** the government offers.

It's called the **home mortgage interest deduction**, and if you're not using it properly, you're leaving **thousands of dollars** on the table every year.

The ultra-wealthy understand how to **use the tax code to their advantage**—and now, you will too.

In this chapter, I'll show you how to:
- ■ **Deduct your mortgage interest legally and maximize your savings.**
- ■ **Take advantage of other homeowner tax benefits.**
- ■ **Use mortgage debt strategically to build wealth while reducing your tax bill.**

What Is the Home Mortgage Interest Deduction?

The **home mortgage interest deduction** allows homeowners to **deduct the interest paid on their mortgage from their taxable income**—lowering the amount of taxes they owe.

📌 Why This Matters:
- ■ **Reduces taxable income** → Less money goes to the IRS.
- ■ **Applies to both primary and secondary homes.**
- ■ **Can be used with home equity loans & refinances.**

💡 Example:
If you paid **$15,000 in mortgage interest** last year and are in the **24% tax bracket**, you'll save **$3,600 in taxes.**

Who Qualifies for the Mortgage Deduction?

To take advantage of this tax break, you must meet the following criteria:

📌 **1. You Must Itemize Your Deductions**

- The mortgage interest deduction **only applies if you itemize** instead of taking the **standard deduction.**
- If your **total deductions exceed the standard deduction**, it's worth itemizing.

📌 **2. Your Mortgage Must Be Secured by Your Home**

- The loan must be for a **primary or secondary residence** (rental properties have different tax rules).
- Your mortgage must be used to **buy, build, or improve your home.**

📌 **3. Your Loan Must Be Below the IRS Limit**

- If you bought your home **before 2017**, you can deduct interest on up to **$1 million in mortgage debt**.
- If you bought your home **after 2017**, the deduction applies only to loans **up to $750,000**.

💡 **Lesson:** If you qualify, you can **reduce your taxable income by thousands** just by owning a home.

How Much Can You Save?

The amount you save depends on:
1. **Your mortgage size** (larger loans = more interest).
2. **Your interest rate** (higher rates = bigger deductions).
3. **Your tax bracket** (higher earners save more).

📌 **Example: A Homeowner Saves $5,400 in Taxes**

- Alex has a **$500,000 mortgage at 5% interest**.
- He pays **$25,000 in mortgage interest** this year.
- He deducts **$25,000 from his taxable income**.
- If he's in the **24% tax bracket**, he saves **$6,000 in taxes**.

💡 **Lesson:** The mortgage deduction gives homeowners a **major financial advantage over renters.**

How to Maximize the Mortgage Deduction

■ Step 1: Itemize If It Saves You More Than the Standard Deduction

The **standard deduction for 2024** is:

- $13,850 for single filers
- $27,700 for married couples

📌 **When to Itemize:**
If your **total deductions (including mortgage interest, property taxes, and donations) exceed the standard deduction**, you should **itemize** to save more.

💡 **Pro Tip: Combine your mortgage deduction with other tax breaks (property taxes, medical expenses, and charitable donations) to increase your total deductions.**

■ Step 2: Deduct Interest on Home Equity Loans & HELOCs

You can deduct interest on **home equity loans** and **HELOCs (Home Equity Lines of Credit)**—but **only if the money is used to improve your home.**

📌 **Example:**

- You take out a **$100,000 HELOC** to remodel your kitchen and bathrooms.
- Your **$5,000 in HELOC interest** is **fully deductible**.

💡 **Warning:** If you use a HELOC for **personal expenses (vacations, cars, credit card debt)**, the interest is NOT deductible.

■ Step 3: Refinance Strategically to Increase Deductions

If you refinance your mortgage, you can **reset your interest payments—extending your deductions.**

📌 **Example:**

- You have **5 years left on your 15-year mortgage.**
- You refinance into a **30-year loan**, lowering your monthly payments.

- Your **new loan restarts the interest deduction**—saving you more on taxes.

💡 **Lesson:** Refinancing can give you **new tax breaks while improving your cash flow.**

🟫 Step 4: Deduct Points Paid on Your Mortgage

If you **paid points** to lower your mortgage interest rate, you can **deduct those points on your taxes.**

📌 How It Works:

- If you **bought a home this year**, you can deduct **all points upfront.**
- If you **refinanced**, you must **spread the deduction over the life of the loan.**

📌 Example: Deducting Mortgage Points

- You pay **$4,000 in points** to lower your mortgage rate.
- If you bought your home this year, you deduct **the full $4,000 immediately.**
- If you refinanced into a **30-year loan**, you deduct **$133 per year for 30 years.**

💡 **Lesson:** Paying points lowers your mortgage rate AND gives you **an additional tax deduction.**

How the Mortgage Deduction Fits into the Buy, Borrow, Die Strategy

📌 **Step 1: Buy a Home Using OPM** → Use an **FHA, VA, or low-down-payment loan** to minimize upfront costs.
📌 **Step 2: Deduct Mortgage Interest Every Year** → Reduce your taxable income by **thousands annually.**
📌 **Step 3: Use Home Equity to Borrow Tax-Free** → Take out a **HELOC or cash-out refinance** instead of selling.
📌 **Step 4: Pass the Home to Your Heirs Tax-Free** → Heirs get a **stepped-up cost basis** (avoiding capital gains taxes).

💡 **Lesson:** The wealthy don't just buy homes—they **use real estate tax strategies to build generational wealth.**

23

The $250,000/$500,000 Home Sale Exemption

Tax-Free Home Sale Jackpot

Imagine selling your home for a massive profit—and **not owing a single penny in taxes.**

That's exactly what the **$250,000/$500,000 Home Sale Exemption** allows you to do.

It's one of the biggest **tax loopholes** in the U.S. tax code, and yet, most homeowners don't fully understand how to **use it correctly to maximize their savings.**

In this chapter, I'll show you how to:
■ **Sell your home and keep up to $500,000 in profit tax-free.**
■ **Qualify for the exemption without triggering IRS penalties.**
■ **Use this strategy repeatedly to build tax-free wealth.**

What Is the Home Sale Exemption?

The **IRS allows homeowners to exclude up to $250,000 (single filers) or $500,000 (married couples) in capital gains** when selling their primary residence.

📌 Why This Matters:
■ **You don't owe capital gains tax on up to $500,000 of profit.**
■ **No need to reinvest the money to qualify.**
■ **You can use this exemption multiple times throughout your life.**

💡 Example:

- You buy a home for **$300,000.**
- You sell it later for **$700,000.**
- Your gain is **$400,000.**

- If you're married, you qualify for the **$500,000 exemption**—so you owe **$0 in capital gains tax.**

Who Qualifies for the $250K/$500K Home Sale Exemption?

To claim this **massive tax break**, you must meet the following **IRS requirements:**

📌 **1. You Must Have Lived in the Home for at Least 2 of the Last 5 Years**

- The **2 years don't have to be consecutive**, but you must have used the home as your **primary residence**.
- If you don't meet this requirement, you may still qualify for a **partial exemption** (more on that later).

📌 **2. You Must Have Owned the Home for at Least 2 Years**

- The ownership period can overlap with the residency period.

📌 **3. You Haven't Used This Exemption in the Last 2 Years**

- You can **only claim the exemption once every two years**.

💡 **Lesson:** If you meet these criteria, you can sell your home and **keep hundreds of thousands of dollars tax-free.**

How Much Can You Save?

📌 **Example 1: Single Homeowner Keeps $250,000 Tax-Free**

- John buys a home for **$200,000** and sells it for **$475,000**.
- His capital gain is **$275,000**.
- He qualifies for the **$250,000 exemption**, so only **$25,000 is taxable**.

📌 **Example 2: Married Couple Keeps $500,000 Tax-Free**

- Sarah and Mike buy a home for **$400,000** and sell it for **$1,000,000**.
- Their capital gain is **$600,000**.
- Because they qualify for the **$500,000 exemption**, only **$100,000 is taxable**.

💡 **Lesson:** The exemption lets you **keep more profit, pay less tax, and grow your wealth faster.**

How to Maximize Your Tax-Free Profits

⬛ Step 1: Keep Track of Home Improvements (To Reduce Your Taxable Gain)

Your **capital gain = Sale Price – (Purchase Price + Improvements).**

📌 **Home Improvements That Reduce Taxable Gains:**

- **Renovations** (kitchen, bathrooms, new roof).
- **Additions** (new rooms, decks, patios).
- **Major repairs** (HVAC, plumbing, foundation).

💡 **Pro Tip:** Keep receipts for **all home upgrades**—they can help you legally reduce your taxable profit.

⬛ Step 2: Time Your Sale to Maximize the Exemption

The **2-year residency rule** is key.

📌 **How to Plan for Maximum Tax-Free Profits:**
✔ If your home has appreciated significantly, **wait until you've met the 2-year rule** before selling.
✔ If you're **not at 2 years yet**, consider **renting it for a short period** while still qualifying.

💡 **Lesson:** Timing matters—**selling too soon could cost you thousands in unnecessary taxes.**

⬛ Step 3: If You Don't Qualify, Use a Partial Exemption

If you don't meet the **full 2-year residency rule**, you might still qualify for a **partial exemption** if you sold due to:
✔ **A job relocation (at least 50 miles away).**
✔ **Health reasons (illness, medical necessity).**
✔ **Unforeseen circumstances (divorce, natural disaster, home damage).**

📌 **Example: A Partial Exemption Saves Thousands**

- Lisa only lived in her home for **1 year before relocating for work.**
- The **$500,000 exemption is reduced to $250,000** (since she lived there for half the required time).
- She still avoids capital gains tax on **$250,000 of her profit.**

💡 **Lesson:** If you don't meet the full rule, **you can still reduce your tax bill.**

⬛ Step 4: Reinvest Tax-Free Profits for More Wealth

Once you sell your home tax-free, don't just **spend the money—use it to grow your wealth.**

📌 **Smart Ways to Reinvest Tax-Free Home Sale Profits:**
⬛ **Buy another home** → Start the exemption cycle again.
⬛ **Use a 1031 Exchange (for rental properties)** → Defer taxes on investment properties.
⬛ **Invest in stocks or REITs** → Let your money grow tax-free inside a **Roth IRA.**
⬛ **Buy income-generating real estate** → Rent it out for **monthly passive income.**

💡 **Lesson:** Don't just **cash out—use tax-free home profits to build even more wealth.**

How This Fits Into the Buy, Borrow, Die Strategy

📌 **Step 1: Buy a Home Using OPM** → Use **low-down-payment loans** (FHA, VA, conventional).
📌 **Step 2: Live in the Home for 2+ Years** → Meet the IRS residency requirement.
📌 **Step 3: Sell for a Huge Profit** → Keep **up to $500,000 tax-free.**
📌 **Step 4: Reinvest the Tax-Free Profits** → Buy another home, invest in assets, or use a 1031 exchange.
📌 **Step 5: Pass Real Estate to Heirs Tax-Free** → They inherit at a **stepped-up cost basis,** avoiding capital gains taxes.

💡 **Lesson:** This strategy lets you **flip homes tax-free every few years, reinvest, and build generational wealth.**

24

Depreciation on Rental Property

Tax-Free Income for Real Estate Investors!

Real estate is one of the **greatest wealth-building tools** in the world.

Not only does it appreciate in value, generate passive income, and provide leverage opportunities, but it also offers **one of the most powerful tax advantages ever created**: **depreciation.**

Depreciation is the reason why wealthy real estate investors **earn tax-free income, pay little to no taxes, and keep more of their profits than the average investor.**

In this chapter, I'll break down how you can:
- **Use depreciation to create tax-free rental income.**
- **Legally deduct property expenses to reduce your tax bill.**
- **Avoid IRS pitfalls and maximize your depreciation strategy.**

What Is Depreciation (And Why Should You Care)?

Depreciation is an IRS rule that allows you to **write off the value of your rental property over time**—even though real estate generally **goes up in value, not down!**

📌 Why This Matters:
- **Lowers your taxable income—without affecting cash flow.**
- **Turns rental profits into "tax-free" income.**
- **Applies even if your property is appreciating.**

💡 Think of depreciation as an IRS loophole that lets you deduct "imaginary" losses—so you keep more of your rental income tax-free.

How Depreciation Works (And How Much You Can Deduct)

The IRS allows you to **depreciate rental properties over 27.5 years**—which means you can deduct **a portion of the home's value from your taxable income every year.**

📌 **Depreciation Formula:**

- (Property Purchase Price − Land Value) ÷ 27.5 = **Annual Depreciation Deduction**

📌 **Example: Depreciating a $500,000 Rental Property**

- You buy a rental property for **$500,000**.
- The land is worth **$100,000**, so the depreciable amount is **$400,000**.
- $400,000 ÷ 27.5 = **$14,545 in annual depreciation deductions.**
- This means you can **reduce your taxable income by $14,545 every year—without actually losing money.**

💡 **Lesson:** Even if your rental property is making money, depreciation can make it look like you're taking a "paper loss"—so you don't pay taxes on your profits.

What Can You Depreciate?

📌 **Depreciation applies to more than just the building.** You can also depreciate:
■ **Improvements & renovations** (new roof, HVAC, plumbing, electrical).
■ **Appliances** (stoves, dishwashers, water heaters).
■ **Furniture (for short-term rentals or furnished units).**

📌 **What You CAN'T Depreciate:**
✗ **The land itself** (land doesn't "wear out").
✗ **Personal-use properties** (only rental properties qualify).

💡 **Lesson:** Any expense that improves or extends the life of the property **can likely be depreciated.**

How Depreciation Turns Rental Income Into Tax-Free Income

Depreciation lets you **write off income that you actually keep.**

📌 **Example: Using Depreciation to Pay Zero Taxes on Rental Income**

- You own a rental property that generates **$20,000 in rental income per year.**
- After expenses, your net rental profit is **$15,000.**
- Thanks to depreciation, you deduct **$14,545** from your taxable income.
- Your "taxable profit" is now just **$455**—meaning you owe almost nothing in taxes!

💡 **Lesson:** Depreciation allows rental investors to **keep more of their income while paying almost nothing in taxes.**

How to Supercharge Depreciation (Cost Segregation Bonus!)

Normally, depreciation is spread out over **27.5 years**—but there's a way to **speed it up and get even bigger tax breaks upfront.**

📌 **Cost Segregation Study:**
A cost segregation study **separates building components** into different categories—allowing you to depreciate some parts of the property **much faster (in 5, 7, or 15 years instead of 27.5).**

📌 **Bonus Depreciation (100% Deduction in Year 1!)**

- The **Tax Cuts and Jobs Act (TCJA)** allows real estate investors to **take 100% bonus depreciation on certain assets in the first year.**
- Instead of spreading out deductions over time, you can **deduct major improvements all at once.**

📌 **Example: How Cost Segregation Saves $50,000 in Taxes**

- A rental property is **purchased for $500,000**.
- A cost segregation study finds that **$200,000** of the property qualifies for **bonus depreciation.**
- Instead of waiting **27.5 years**, the investor deducts **$200,000 in Year 1.**

- If the investor is in the **35% tax bracket**, this saves **$70,000 in taxes immediately.**

📍 **Lesson:** If you own **multiple rental properties**, a cost segregation study can provide **massive upfront tax benefits.**

Avoiding Depreciation Recapture (How to Keep Your Tax Savings Forever)

The IRS loves giving tax breaks—but **they also love taking them back.**

When you sell a rental property, the IRS may charge **depreciation recapture tax**—which means they **tax the depreciation deductions you've taken over the years.**

📌 **How to Avoid Depreciation Recapture:**
⬛ **Use a 1031 Exchange** → Defer taxes by reinvesting into another rental property.
⬛ **Hold the Property Until Death** → Heirs get a **stepped-up cost basis**, wiping out recapture taxes.
⬛ **Keep Refinancing Instead of Selling** → Use your home equity tax-free instead of selling.

📍 **Lesson:** Never sell rental properties without a plan—**depreciation recapture can be avoided with the right strategy.**

How Depreciation Fits into the Buy, Borrow, Die Strategy

📌 **Step 1: Buy a Rental Property Using OPM** → Use **low-interest loans** and **minimal down payments.**
📌 **Step 2: Depreciate the Property** → Write off **tens of thousands of dollars** in paper losses.
📌 **Step 3: Keep Collecting Tax-Free Income** → Rental profits are **offset by depreciation deductions.**
📌 **Step 4: Refinance Instead of Selling** → Take out **cash tax-free** without triggering recapture.
📌 **Step 5: Pass the Property to Heirs Tax-Free** → Stepped-up cost basis **eliminates depreciation recapture taxes.**

📍 **Lesson:** The wealthy don't sell real estate—they **use depreciation, refinance, and pass it down tax-free.**

25

Cost Segregation

Boosting Tax-Free Income for Real Estate Investors

If you own rental properties, you probably already know about **depreciation**—the powerful tax strategy that lets you deduct a portion of your property's value over 27.5 years.

But what if I told you that you **don't have to wait nearly three decades to get your tax savings?**

With **cost segregation**, you can **accelerate your depreciation deductions**—allowing you to write off a huge portion of your investment **in the first few years instead of spreading it out over time.**

This is how **the wealthiest real estate investors reduce their taxable income to nearly zero—while keeping all their rental profits tax-free.**

In this chapter, I'll show you how cost segregation works, who should use it, and how you can legally **wipe out your tax bill using one of the IRS's biggest real estate loopholes.**

What Is Cost Segregation?

Cost segregation is an advanced tax strategy that allows real estate investors to **break down their property into different asset categories**—so they can depreciate certain parts of the building **much faster** than the standard 27.5-year timeline.

📌 Why This Matters:
■ **Maximizes tax deductions in the early years of ownership.**
■ **Generates more tax-free rental income.**
■ **Improves cash flow by reducing taxable income.**
■ **Works for both residential and commercial properties.**

💡 Think of cost segregation as a way to "fast-track" your tax savings—allowing you to **deduct a massive portion of your property's value upfront instead of waiting decades.**

How Cost Segregation Works

When you buy a property, the IRS allows you to **depreciate different components of the building at different speeds.**

Depreciation Timelines Without Cost Segregation

- **Buildings (Structure)** → Depreciated over **27.5 years** (residential) or **39 years** (commercial).
- **Land → Not depreciable.**

📌 But with cost segregation, you can separate parts of the building into faster depreciation schedules:

Asset Category	Depreciation Timeline
Appliances, Cabinets, Carpeting, Flooring	5 years
HVAC, Plumbing, Electrical Systems	7 years
Sidewalks, Driveways, Landscaping	15 years

💡 Instead of waiting 27.5 years, you can claim big deductions on these assets in just 5-15 years!

How Much Can Cost Segregation Save You?

📌 **Example: Accelerating Depreciation on a $1 Million Property**

- You buy a rental property for **$1,000,000**.
- Without cost segregation, you can only depreciate the building over **27.5 years** → **$36,363 per year in deductions.**
- But a cost segregation study finds that **30% of the property** qualifies for **5- and 15-year depreciation**.
- This means you can deduct **$300,000** in **the first few years** instead of waiting decades.

💡 **Lesson:** If you're making big rental profits, cost segregation lets you **wipe out your taxable income faster—so you pay zero taxes.**

Bonus Depreciation: Supercharging Your Tax Savings

With **bonus depreciation**, you can **write off 100% of certain property costs in the first year** instead of spreading them out over time.

📌 How It Works:

- Before 2017, cost segregation allowed you to **speed up deductions—but you still had to wait a few years**.
- Thanks to the **2017 Tax Cuts and Jobs Act (TCJA)**, you can **now deduct 100% of qualified property expenses in Year 1!**

📌 Example: Using Bonus Depreciation to Write Off $200,000 Immediately

- A cost segregation study finds **$200,000 of your $1 million rental property** qualifies for **bonus depreciation**.
- Instead of waiting 5-15 years, you deduct **the full $200,000 in the first year**.
- If you're in the **37% tax bracket**, that's an immediate **$74,000 tax savings!**

💡 **Lesson:** Bonus depreciation allows real estate investors to **wipe out massive chunks of their tax bill instantly**.

Who Should Use Cost Segregation?

Cost segregation is best for **high-income real estate investors** who want to **maximize their tax savings upfront**.

📌 Best Candidates for Cost Segregation:
■ **Investors who own rental properties worth $500,000+** (best for larger investments).
■ **Real estate professionals** (they get extra tax benefits from depreciation).
■ **Anyone with big rental income who wants to reduce their tax bill.**

📌 Not Ideal For:
✖ **Small rental properties ($100K or less).**
✖ **Short-term property owners (under 2-3 years).**
✖ **Investors with little taxable income** (cost segregation works best if you need tax breaks).

💡 **Lesson:** If you're making money from rental properties, **cost segregation can help you keep more of it.**

How to Get a Cost Segregation Study (And Is It Worth It?)

To use cost segregation, you need a **cost segregation study**—a detailed report done by tax professionals and engineers that identifies which parts of your building qualify for **accelerated depreciation**.

📌 **Steps to Get a Cost Segregation Study:**
1. **Hire a cost segregation specialist** (tax pros and engineers work together).
2. **They break down your property into different asset categories** (5-year, 7-year, 15-year).
3. **You claim faster depreciation deductions on your tax return.**

📌 **Cost of a Study:**

- **$5,000 to $15,000** (but worth it for larger properties).

📌 **When It's Worth It:**

- If your property is worth **$500,000+**, a cost segregation study can **save you $50,000+ in taxes**—making it a smart investment.

💡 **Lesson:** Cost segregation isn't free—but for serious investors, the tax savings can be **massive.**

How Cost Segregation Fits into the Buy, Borrow, Die Strategy

📌 **Step 1: Buy Rental Properties Using OPM** → Use **low-down-payment loans** to acquire real estate.
📌 **Step 2: Use Cost Segregation to Maximize Tax-Free Income** → Write off a **huge portion of the purchase price upfront.**
📌 **Step 3: Keep Collecting Tax-Free Rental Income** → Let depreciation **wipe out your taxable profits.**
📌 **Step 4: Refinance Instead of Selling** → Pull out cash tax-free without paying depreciation recapture.
📌 **Step 5: Pass the Property to Heirs Tax-Free** → Heirs get a **stepped-up cost basis**, avoiding depreciation recapture.

💡 **Lesson:** Cost segregation helps real estate investors **pay less in taxes while keeping more cash flow for future investments.**

26

Bonus Depreciation

Supercharging Tax-Free Income for Real Estate Investors

If you think depreciation is powerful, wait until you learn about bonus depreciation—the ultimate real estate tax hack.

For decades, real estate investors have used depreciation to reduce their taxable income, but the standard 27.5-year schedule meant it took a long time to get the full benefit.

That all changed with the 2017 Tax Cuts and Jobs Act (TCJA), which introduced 100% bonus depreciation, allowing investors to write off massive amounts in the first year instead of waiting decades.

This is how the wealthiest investors pay little to no taxes—while keeping their rental profits tax-free.

In this chapter, I'll show you how bonus depreciation works, how to use it legally, and how to supercharge your tax-free real estate income.

What Is Bonus Depreciation?

Bonus depreciation allows real estate investors to immediately deduct 100% of certain property costs in the first year, instead of spreading them out over decades.

📌 Why This Matters:
■ Turns rental income into tax-free cash flow.
■ Provides massive upfront tax savings (instead of waiting 27.5 years).
■ Works for both residential and commercial properties.
■ Can be combined with cost segregation for even bigger tax breaks.

💡 Think of bonus depreciation as a "turbocharged" version of regular depreciation—it lets you claim huge deductions upfront, keeping more of your money in your pocket today.

How Bonus Depreciation Works

Normally, real estate depreciation follows this schedule:

- Buildings → 27.5 years (residential) / 39 years (commercial).
- Land → Not depreciable.
- Appliances, HVAC, Carpeting, Fixtures → Depreciated over 5-15 years.

But with bonus depreciation, you can fully deduct these 5-15 year items in Year 1 instead of waiting.

📌 Example: Bonus Depreciation on a $1M Rental Property

- You buy a $1,000,000 rental property.
- A cost segregation study finds that $300,000 of the property qualifies for 5, 7, and 15-year depreciation schedules.
- Instead of waiting 5-15 years, you deduct the full $300,000 immediately in Year 1.
- If you're in the 35% tax bracket, you just saved $105,000 in taxes—instantly.

💡 Lesson: Bonus depreciation lets you claim huge tax savings upfront, rather than waiting years for small deductions.

What Qualifies for Bonus Depreciation?

Not every part of a rental property qualifies for bonus depreciation—but a lot of it does.

📌 Bonus Depreciation Applies To:
■ Personal Property → Appliances, furniture, cabinets, carpets, fixtures.
■ Land Improvements → Driveways, fences, sidewalks, landscaping.
■ HVAC, Electrical, Plumbing Systems → If separated in a cost segregation study.
■ Short-Term Rental Properties (Airbnb, VRBO) → If classified as a business.

📌 Bonus Depreciation Does NOT Apply To:
✗ The building itself (must follow 27.5-year depreciation).
✗ Land (never depreciable).

💡 Lesson: The key to unlocking bonus depreciation is a cost segregation study—which identifies all the parts of the property that qualify for faster write-offs.

How to Maximize Bonus Depreciation

■ Step 1: Get a Cost Segregation Study

A cost segregation study breaks down your property into different asset classes—allowing you to maximize your bonus depreciation deductions.

📌 Why It's Worth It:

- Cost segregation studies cost $5,000 to $15,000.
- But they often generate $50,000+ in tax savings per property.

💡 Pro Tip: If your rental property is worth $500,000+, a cost segregation study is almost always worth it.

■ Step 2: Use Bonus Depreciation on New Purchases & Improvements

Bonus depreciation applies not just to new properties, but also to renovations and upgrades.

📌 Example: Using Bonus Depreciation for a Renovation

- You buy $50,000 worth of new appliances, HVAC, and flooring.
- Instead of depreciating over 5-15 years, you deduct the full $50,000 in Year 1.

💡 Lesson: Any major property improvements can also qualify for bonus depreciation—giving you another way to reduce taxes.

■ Step 3: Combine Bonus Depreciation with a 1031 Exchange

- If you sell a property and use a 1031 Exchange to defer taxes, you can also use bonus depreciation on the new property.
- This means you can keep rolling your profits forward, avoiding taxes indefinitely.

📌 Example: Combining a 1031 Exchange with Bonus Depreciation

- You sell a rental property for $1 million.
- Instead of paying capital gains tax, you do a 1031 Exchange and buy another property.
- You use bonus depreciation on the new property to wipe out taxable income for years.

📍 Lesson: Never sell a property without a tax plan—use bonus depreciation and 1031 exchanges together for maximum savings.

Who Should Use Bonus Depreciation?

📌 Best Candidates for Bonus Depreciation:
■ Real estate investors with high rental income (who want to eliminate taxes).
■ Short-term rental owners (Airbnb, VRBO) (who qualify for business tax treatment).
■ Investors planning renovations (who want to deduct upgrades immediately).
■ Anyone buying rental properties worth $500,000+ (who can benefit from cost segregation).

📌 Not Ideal For:
✘ Investors with little taxable income (won't need extra deductions).
✘ Flippers (who don't hold properties long enough).
✘ People who don't plan to own real estate long-term.

📍 Lesson: Bonus depreciation is best for long-term real estate investors looking to maximize tax-free cash flow.

How Bonus Depreciation Fits into the Buy, Borrow, Die Strategy

📌 Step 1: Buy Rental Properties Using OPM → Use low-interest loans to acquire real estate.
📌 Step 2: Use Cost Segregation & Bonus Depreciation → Deduct huge amounts in Year 1.
📌 Step 3: Keep Collecting Tax-Free Rental Income → Let depreciation offset taxable profits.
📌 Step 4: Refinance Instead of Selling → Take out cash tax-free without triggering taxes.
📌 Step 5: Pass the Property to Heirs Tax-Free → They inherit at a stepped-up cost basis, eliminating depreciation recapture.

📍 Lesson: Bonus depreciation lets investors pay zero taxes on rental income while growing their portfolio tax-free.

27

Business Ownership and Rental Income

Buy One to Live In and One to Rent

Owning real estate is one of the most powerful wealth-building strategies available.

But what if you could take it even further?

What if you could own a home, own a rental property, AND use business tax strategies to reduce your tax bill to almost zero?

That's exactly what the wealthy do—they don't just buy real estate, they combine rental income with business ownership to maximize tax-free wealth.

In this chapter, I'll show you how to:
■ Buy one property to live in and one to rent—without spending all your cash.
■ Use business ownership to maximize real estate tax deductions.
■ Create multiple income streams while paying little to no taxes.

Step 1: Buy One to Live In and One to Rent (With Minimal Cash Down)

Most people think they need a huge down payment to buy real estate—but the truth is, you can acquire multiple properties with little money out of pocket.

📌 Here's How to Do It:
1. Buy a primary residence using a low-down-payment loan (FHA, VA, or Conventional 3%).
2. Use a separate loan to buy a rental property.
3. House-hack your primary home (rent out extra rooms or a basement).
4. Use the rental property's income to cover your mortgage payments.

📌 Example: How to Own Two Properties with Just $20,000 Down

- You buy a $400,000 primary home with an FHA loan (3.5% down = $14,000).
- You buy a $300,000 rental property with a 15% down investor loan ($45,000 down).
- Your total investment = $59,000 (but you can use seller credits and financing to reduce this).
- Your rental property brings in $2,500/month in rent, covering the mortgage.

💡 Lesson: You don't need millions to own multiple properties—you just need the right financing strategy.

Step 2: Turn Your Real Estate Portfolio into a Business

The wealthy don't own rental properties in their personal name—they own them through an LLC or S-Corp to get even bigger tax benefits.

📌 Why You Should Own Rentals in a Business Entity:
■ Reduces personal liability (protects your assets).
■ Allows you to deduct more business expenses.
■ Creates additional tax advantages (business tax write-offs).

💡 Pro Tip: If you own multiple properties, putting them under an LLC allows you to write off expenses like travel, home office costs, and professional services.

Step 3: Use Business Tax Deductions to Reduce Rental Income Taxes

Once you treat your rental properties like a business, you can start using business tax deductions to lower your taxable rental income.

📌 Tax-Deductible Expenses for Landlords & Real Estate Businesses:
■ Mortgage interest
■ Property taxes
■ Insurance
■ Repairs & maintenance
■ Property management fees
■ Legal & accounting fees

■ Travel expenses related to rental property
■ Depreciation (including bonus depreciation!)

📌 Example: How Business Tax Write-Offs Save $10,000 in Taxes

- You make $40,000 per year from rental income.
- After expenses, your net rental profit is $30,000.
- You use bonus depreciation to write off $15,000.
- Your taxable income drops to $15,000.
- If you're in the 25% tax bracket, you just saved $3,750 in taxes!

💡 Lesson: Owning rental properties through a business allows you to legally reduce your taxable income—keeping more rental profits tax-free.

Step 4: Use a Home Office Deduction to Reduce Taxes Even More

If you own a rental property AND a business, you can claim a home office deduction, even if your business is just managing your own properties.

📌 How the Home Office Deduction Works:

- If you use 10% of your home as an office, you can deduct 10% of your rent/mortgage, utilities, and home expenses.
- This deduction reduces your taxable income, even if you're already writing off rental expenses.

📌 Example: Using a Home Office Deduction to Save $3,000 in Taxes

- Your total home costs (rent, utilities, internet, etc.) = $30,000 per year.
- Your home office takes up 10% of your home → You can deduct $3,000.
- This deduction reduces your taxable business income, saving you up to $1,000 in taxes.

💡 Lesson: If you own rental properties and manage them yourself, you should be taking a home office deduction to reduce your tax bill even further.

Step 5: House-Hack for Even More Tax-Free Income

Want to live for free while owning real estate?

House hacking is the strategy of living in one part of your home and renting out the other parts to cover your mortgage.

📌 Ways to House-Hack:
■ Buy a multi-unit property (duplex, triplex, or fourplex).
■ Rent out extra rooms on Airbnb.
■ Live in one unit, rent the others to tenants.

📌 Example: How House-Hacking Eliminates Your Housing Costs

- You buy a $500,000 duplex with an FHA loan (3.5% down).
- Your total mortgage payment = $3,000/month.
- You rent out the other unit for $2,500/month.
- Your net housing cost = just $500/month instead of $3,000.

💡 Lesson: House hacking is one of the easiest ways to build real estate wealth without using your own money.

How This Fits Into the Buy, Borrow, Die Strategy

📌 Step 1: Buy a Home and a Rental Property Using OPM → Use low-down-payment loans to acquire both.
📌 Step 2: Set Up an LLC or S-Corp → Protect assets and increase tax deductions.
📌 Step 3: Use Business Tax Deductions → Write off mortgage interest, home office, travel, and depreciation.
📌 Step 4: House-Hack to Live for Free → Reduce your personal living expenses to almost zero.
📌 Step 5: Refinance Instead of Selling → Pull out cash tax-free without triggering capital gains taxes.

💡 Lesson: Combining real estate and business ownership lets you pay fewer taxes, live for free, and build long-term wealth.

28

Real Estate Professional Status

The "Secret Sauce" to Pay No Taxes

If you're serious about building wealth through real estate, you need to know about Real Estate Professional Status (REPS).

This is one of the biggest loopholes in the U.S. tax code—a strategy that allows investors to use rental property losses to offset ALL of their income, not just rental profits.

That's right—you can use real estate losses to wipe out taxes on your salary, business income, and even stock market gains!

This is how wealthy investors pay zero taxes while growing massive real estate portfolios.

In this chapter, I'll show you:
■ How REPS lets you pay NO taxes legally.
■ Who qualifies as a Real Estate Professional (and who doesn't).
■ The step-by-step process to claim REPS and maximize tax savings.

What Is Real Estate Professional Status (REPS)?

Most real estate investors are considered passive investors by the IRS.

This means they can only use rental property losses to offset rental income—not other types of income.

📌 BUT… If you qualify for REPS, rental losses can offset ALL income—including:
■ W-2 salary
■ Business income (from an LLC, S-Corp, or sole proprietorship)
■ Capital gains from stocks, crypto, and real estate sales

💡 This means real estate investors with REPS can take massive tax deductions—often paying ZERO federal income taxes.

How Much Can You Save with REPS?

📌 Example 1: High-Income Earner Uses REPS to Pay No Taxes

- Lisa earns $250,000 per year as a business owner.
- She owns 3 rental properties and qualifies as a Real Estate Professional.
- She claims $100,000 in depreciation and property expenses.
- She offsets $100,000 of her business income → Her taxable income drops to $150,000.
- If she's in the 35% tax bracket, she just saved $35,000 in taxes.

📌 Example 2: REPS Eliminates Taxes for a Married Couple

- John makes $200,000 per year as a software engineer.
- His wife, Sarah, manages their rental portfolio full-time and qualifies for REPS.
- Their rental properties generate $60,000 in paper losses (depreciation, expenses).
- They deduct the full $60,000 from John's salary → Their taxable income drops to $140,000.
- They save $18,000+ in taxes—without losing a single dollar.

💡 Lesson: REPS lets investors use paper losses to legally avoid paying income taxes.

How to Qualify for Real Estate Professional Status

The IRS has strict rules for who qualifies as a Real Estate Professional.

To claim REPS, you must meet two key tests:

■ Test #1: 750-Hour Rule

You must work at least 750 hours per year (about 15 hours per week) in real estate-related activities.

📌 Qualifying Real Estate Activities:
■ Managing rental properties
■ Negotiating leases
■ Screening tenants

■ Supervising renovations and repairs
■ Marketing and advertising rentals

💡 If you have a full-time W-2 job, it's almost impossible to meet this requirement—unless your spouse qualifies instead.

■ Test #2: More Than 50% of Your Working Hours Must Be in Real Estate

If you work another job, you must spend more time on real estate than your job to qualify for REPS.

📌 Example: Who Qualifies?
✔ Yes: A stay-at-home spouse managing properties full-time.
✔ Yes: A self-employed person spending 800+ hours a year on rentals.
✖ No: A full-time engineer who only spends 500 hours a year on real estate.

💡 Lesson: If you have a full-time W-2 job, your best bet is for your spouse to qualify for REPS while you earn the salary.

Step-by-Step Guide to Claiming REPS and Avoiding Taxes

■ Step 1: Keep Detailed Records of Your Time

The IRS doesn't automatically believe you qualify—you must prove your hours with records.

📌 Ways to Track REPS Hours:

- Google Calendar or Excel Spreadsheet → Log time spent managing properties.
- Property management software → Keep track of tenant interactions, repairs, and marketing.
- Emails, calls, invoices → Save receipts and communications related to rental activities.

💡 Pro Tip: If you get audited, the IRS will ask for proof—so track everything!

🟥 Step 2: Use Cost Segregation and Bonus Depreciation for Maximum Write-Offs

If you qualify for REPS, you can use cost segregation and bonus depreciation to take huge tax deductions.

📌 Example: Supercharging Tax Savings with REPS + Cost Segregation

- You buy a $1 million rental property.
- A cost segregation study finds that $300,000 qualifies for bonus depreciation.
- You deduct $300,000 in Year 1, wiping out your entire taxable income.
- If you're in the 37% tax bracket, you just saved $111,000 in taxes.

💡 Lesson: REPS + Bonus Depreciation = No Taxes + More Money to Reinvest.

🟥 Step 3: File Your Taxes Correctly

To claim REPS, you must:
📌 Report rental losses on IRS Form 1040, Schedule E.
📌 Attach Form 8582 (Passive Activity Loss Limitations) to prove you qualify.

💡 Pro Tip: Work with a CPA who specializes in real estate tax strategies—they can help you avoid IRS mistakes.

How REPS Fits Into the Buy, Borrow, Die Strategy

📌 Step 1: Buy Rental Properties Using OPM → Use low-down-payment loans to acquire real estate.
📌 Step 2: Qualify for REPS → Prove 750+ hours and more than 50% of your time is in real estate.
📌 Step 3: Use Cost Segregation & Bonus Depreciation → Write off huge amounts in Year 1.
📌 Step 4: Offset All Income (Including W-2 or Business Income) → Pay little to no taxes.
📌 Step 5: Refinance Instead of Selling → Pull out cash tax-free without triggering capital gains taxes.
📌 Step 6: Pass the Property to Heirs Tax-Free → They inherit at a stepped-up cost basis, eliminating depreciation recapture.

💡 Lesson: REPS allows real estate investors to turn rental properties into tax-free income machines.

29

The Home Office Deduction

Your Tax-Saving Super Weapon

If you're managing rental properties, running a business, or even working part-time from home, you could be sitting on one of the most overlooked tax deductions in the IRS rulebook:

📌 The Home Office Deduction.

This deduction lets you write off a portion of your home expenses—effectively making part of your rent or mortgage tax-deductible.

The best part? You don't even need to own a business to claim it.

In this chapter, I'll show you:
■ Who qualifies for the home office deduction.
■ How to calculate your deduction (without triggering an audit).
■ How real estate investors can use it to reduce rental income taxes.

How the Home Office Deduction Works

The IRS allows self-employed individuals, business owners, and rental property managers to deduct a portion of their rent, utilities, internet, and other home expenses if they use part of their home exclusively for business.

📌 Why This Matters:
■ Reduces your taxable income, saving you money.
■ Allows you to deduct rent/mortgage, utilities, and home-related expenses.
■ Works for real estate investors managing rental properties.

💡 Lesson: If you have a dedicated workspace at home, you could be missing out on a huge tax break!

Who Qualifies for the Home Office Deduction?

To claim this deduction, you must meet two IRS requirements:

🔲 1. Exclusive and Regular Use

- Your home office must be used only for business purposes—not as a guest room, gym, or personal space.
- It doesn't have to be an entire room, but it must be a clearly defined workspace.

📌 Examples of Qualifying Spaces:
✔ A separate room used only for business.
✔ A desk in a dedicated corner of your home.
✔ A converted garage or basement office.

📌 Examples of Non-Qualifying Spaces:
✘ Your dining room table (if used for meals too).
✘ A bedroom that doubles as a guest room.
✘ A shared family workspace.

💡 Pro Tip: If you're audited, the IRS may check whether your home office is exclusively business-related—so keep it strictly professional.

🔲 2. Principal Place of Business

- Your home office must be the main place where you conduct business.
- This includes administrative work, calls, bookkeeping, and property management.
- Even if you have an outside office, you can still qualify if your home office is your primary work location.

📌 Who Can Claim This Deduction?
✔ Self-employed business owners (LLCs, S-Corps, freelancers).
✔ Real estate investors managing their own properties.
✔ Real estate professionals who qualify for REPS.

📌 Who Can't Claim It?
✘ W-2 employees who work from home (unless required by an employer with no office provided).

💡 Lesson: If you work for yourself or manage rental properties, you should be claiming this deduction.

How Much Can You Deduct?

There are two ways to calculate the home office deduction:

Method #1: The Simplified Option (Easy & Quick)

- Deduct $5 per square foot of your home office.
- Maximum deduction = $1,500 per year (300 sq ft max).
- No receipts or detailed tracking required.

📌 Example:

- You use a 200 sq ft home office.
- 200 sq ft × $5 = $1,000 deduction.

💡 Best For: Small home offices or people who want a quick, hassle-free deduction.

Method #2: The Detailed Method (Bigger Deduction Potential)

- Deduct a percentage of your total home expenses (mortgage, rent, utilities, property taxes, internet, insurance, and maintenance).
- Percentage = Home office square footage ÷ Total home square footage.

📌 Example: A Landlord Saves $3,000 in Taxes with the Detailed Method

- Total home size = 2,000 sq ft.
- Home office size = 400 sq ft (20% of home).
- Total annual home expenses (rent, utilities, insurance, maintenance) = $30,000.
- 20% of $30,000 = $6,000 deduction.
- If you're in the 25% tax bracket, you save $1,500 in taxes!

💡 Best For: People with larger home offices and higher home expenses.

How Real Estate Investors Can Use the Home Office Deduction

If you own rental properties, you can claim the home office deduction even if you're not a full-time real estate professional.

📌 Example: A Rental Property Investor Uses the Home Office Deduction

- Sarah owns three rental properties and manages them herself.
- She works from a 250 sq ft office in her home.
- She deducts $5,000 per year in home office expenses.
- This deduction reduces her rental income taxes—keeping more cash in her pocket.

💡 Lesson: If you actively manage rental properties, you should be claiming the home office deduction to offset rental income taxes.

How the Home Office Deduction Fits into the Buy, Borrow, Die Strategy

📌 Step 1: Buy Real Estate & Set Up an LLC → Start treating your rentals like a business.
📌 Step 2: Deduct Home Office Expenses → Reduce taxable rental income using the home office deduction.
📌 Step 3: Use Depreciation & Bonus Depreciation → Lower taxes even further.
📌 Step 4: Keep Rental Profits Tax-Free → Avoid unnecessary taxes while growing your portfolio.
📌 Step 5: Pass Properties to Heirs Tax-Free → Use a stepped-up cost basis to eliminate capital gains taxes.

💡 Lesson: The home office deduction is a simple but powerful way to reduce taxes while managing real estate.

Avoiding IRS Red Flags (How to Claim the Deduction Safely)

The IRS scrutinizes home office deductions, so you need to follow the rules carefully.

📌 **Best Practices to Avoid an Audit:**
✔ Use a clearly defined office space (not your couch or kitchen table).
✔ Track your home office expenses with receipts and logs.
✔ Take photos of your office setup (for proof if audited).
✔ Keep a daily or weekly log of work-related activities.
✔ If unsure, consult a tax professional before filing.

💡 Lesson: As long as you follow IRS guidelines, the home office deduction is 100% legal and extremely valuable.

30

The Augusta Rule

Unlocking Tax-Free Income Through Short-Term Rentals

Imagine legally earning thousands of dollars in rental income every year—without paying a single penny in taxes.

That's exactly what the Augusta Rule allows you to do.

Named after Augusta, Georgia, where wealthy homeowners rent out their mansions during the Masters golf tournament completely tax-free, this loophole lets any homeowner in the U.S. rent out their home for up to 14 days per year—without reporting it to the IRS.

Most people never take advantage of this rule, but real estate investors and business owners can use it to generate tax-free rental income every year.

In this chapter, I'll show you:
■ How the Augusta Rule works (and how to legally avoid taxes on rental income).
■ How to use it for short-term rentals (Airbnb, VRBO, corporate rentals).
■ How business owners can rent their own home to their business—completely tax-free.

What Is the Augusta Rule?

📌 The Augusta Rule (IRC Section 280A) allows homeowners to rent out their home for up to 14 days per year and exclude that income from taxes.

📌 Why This Matters:
■ Rental income is completely tax-free (not reported to the IRS).
■ You don't have to own a rental property to qualify.
■ Works for Airbnb, vacation rentals, business use, and corporate events.

💡 Lesson: The Augusta Rule is a powerful tax strategy that turns short-term rentals into tax-free income.

How Much Can You Earn Tax-Free with the Augusta Rule?

The IRS does not cap how much you can charge per night—only that you can't rent out your home for more than 14 days per year.

📌 Example: Homeowner Makes $14,000 Tax-Free

- You rent out your home for $1,000 per night during a major event (like the Super Bowl or Masters Tournament).
- You rent it out for 14 nights per year → $14,000 in tax-free rental income.
- You pay zero taxes on that $14,000!

💡 Lesson: The higher your rental rate, the more tax-free money you can make.

Who Can Use the Augusta Rule?

The Augusta Rule applies to any homeowner who:
✔ Owns a primary residence or vacation home in the U.S.
✔ Rents it out for 14 days or fewer per year.
✔ Charges a fair market rental rate for the area.

📌 Who Can't Use It?
✘ If you rent your home for more than 14 days, you must report all rental income.
✘ If you rent it for $0 (or way below market rate), the IRS may deny your exemption.

💡 Lesson: As long as you limit rentals to 14 days and charge fair rates, you qualify for tax-free income.

How to Use the Augusta Rule for Airbnb & Short-Term Rentals

The easiest way to apply the Augusta Rule is by renting your home for short-term stays—especially during peak seasons, major events, or holidays.

📌 Examples of Using the Augusta Rule for Short-Term Rentals:
✔ Hosting Airbnb guests for 14 days per year at premium rates.
✔ Renting your vacation home during peak season (without triggering rental taxes).
✔ Offering corporate housing for executives visiting your area.

📌 Example: Making $10,000 in Tax-Free Airbnb Income

- You own a home near a major college football stadium.
- You list it on Airbnb for $1,000 per night during home games.
- You rent it out for 10 nights per year → Earn $10,000 tax-free!

💡 Lesson: If you have a home in a high-demand area, the Augusta Rule lets you legally keep all rental profits tax-free.

How Business Owners Can Use the Augusta Rule for Even Bigger Tax Savings

📌 If you own a business, you can rent your home to your business tax-free!

How It Works:

1️⃣ Your business rents your home for meetings, team retreats, or company events.
2️⃣ Your business deducts the rental expense as a business expense.
3️⃣ You receive the rental income tax-free under the Augusta Rule.
4️⃣ You keep 100% of the rental money—while reducing business taxes.

📌 Example: A Business Owner Uses the Augusta Rule for $21,000 in Tax Savings

- John owns an LLC and works from home.
- His LLC rents his home for monthly business meetings (12 times per year, $1,750 per meeting).
- The LLC deducts $21,000 as a business expense.
- John keeps the $21,000 rental income tax-free.

💡 Lesson: Business owners can legally shift money from their business to personal income—without paying taxes.

How to Use the Augusta Rule the Right Way (and Avoid IRS Audits)

The IRS allows this deduction as long as you follow the rules carefully.

📌 Best Practices to Stay Compliant:
✔ Charge fair market rental rates (check Airbnb or hotel prices in your area).
✔ Sign a rental agreement between you and your business (if using it for corporate meetings).
✔ Document rental payments with receipts and invoices.
✔ Limit rentals to 14 days or fewer per year—no exceptions.
✔ If using for business, keep meeting agendas and records.

💡 Lesson: The Augusta Rule is 100% legal, but you must document everything to protect yourself in case of an IRS audit.

How the Augusta Rule Fits Into the Buy, Borrow, Die Strategy

📌 Step 1: Buy a Home or Vacation Property → Own a primary residence or second home.
📌 Step 2: Use the Augusta Rule to Rent It Out for 14 Days Tax-Free → Airbnb, business meetings, or corporate stays.
📌 Step 3: Generate Up to $50,000 Tax-Free → If your home is in a high-demand area.
📌 Step 4: Use the Tax-Free Money to Invest → Buy more real estate, fund renovations, or pay down mortgages.
📌 Step 5: Keep Scaling Without Paying Taxes → Continue leveraging tax-free rental income every year.

💡 Lesson: The Augusta Rule allows homeowners to turn their property into a tax-free income machine.

31

The Short-Term Rentals Loophole

A Powerful Tool for Tax Savings

What if I told you that you could own rental properties, collect thousands in tax-free income, and legally pay ZERO income taxes—without needing Real Estate Professional Status (REPS)?

That's exactly what the Short-Term Rental (STR) Loophole allows you to do.

This little-known IRS loophole makes short-term rentals (Airbnb, VRBO, and vacation rentals) one of the most tax-efficient real estate strategies available today.

In this chapter, I'll show you:
■ How the STR loophole lets you deduct massive rental losses against W-2 and business income.
■ How to qualify (without meeting the strict REPS rules).
■ How to use depreciation and tax deductions to create tax-free rental income.

How the Short-Term Rental Loophole Works

Normally, rental income is considered passive income—meaning rental losses can't be used to offset your W-2 or business income unless you qualify as a Real Estate Professional (REPS).

📌 BUT... If you own a short-term rental and meet IRS requirements, it is considered an ACTIVE business—allowing you to deduct losses against ALL other income.

📌 Why This Matters:
■ You don't need REPS to use rental losses to offset W-2 or business income.
■ Short-term rental owners can take massive tax deductions (including depreciation).
■ You can legally use rental losses to reduce taxable income and pay little to no taxes.

💡 Lesson: The STR loophole allows investors to use tax-free rental income while avoiding the strict 750-hour rule of REPS.

How Much Can You Save?

📌 Example: Using the STR Loophole to Wipe Out $40,000 in Taxes

- Sarah is a doctor earning $300,000 per year (high-income earner).
- She buys an Airbnb property for $500,000 and rents it out on weekends.
- A cost segregation study finds that she can claim $150,000 in bonus depreciation.
- Because her STR qualifies as an active business, she deducts $150,000 against her W-2 income.
- Her taxable income drops to $150,000, saving her $40,000+ in taxes.

💡 Lesson: STR investors can use depreciation and deductions to offset not just rental income, but ALL income.

Who Qualifies for the STR Loophole?

To use the STR loophole, you must meet two IRS requirements:

🔲 1. The "Average Stay" Test

To be considered an active business (instead of a passive rental property), the IRS requires that:

📌 The average stay per guest is 7 days or less OR 30 days or less with significant services provided (cleaning, meals, concierge).

✔ Yes: Airbnb, VRBO, vacation rentals with stays under 7 days.
✔ Yes: Corporate housing that includes services.
✘ No: Traditional long-term rentals with leases over 30 days.

💡 Lesson: If your property has short-term guests, it can qualify as an active business—allowing you to deduct losses against other income.

🔲 2. The "Material Participation" Test

Unlike REPS, you don't need 750 hours—but you must materially participate in managing the property.

📌 You must meet ONE of these three tests:

✔ 1. Spend 500+ hours per year managing the property.
✔ 2. Spend 100+ hours AND more time than anyone else (including property managers).
✔ 3. Manage the property yourself and perform ALL significant work.

💡 Lesson: If you actively manage your short-term rental, you qualify for massive tax benefits—even with a full-time job.

How to Use the STR Loophole to Pay Zero Taxes

◼ Step 1: Buy a Short-Term Rental in a High-Demand Area

- Look for Airbnb-friendly cities with high nightly rates.
- Consider properties near beaches, ski resorts, theme parks, national parks, or downtown hubs.

📌 Best STR Markets (2024):
✔ Orlando, FL (Disney World).
✔ Scottsdale, AZ (golf, spring training).
✔ Nashville, TN (music, nightlife).
✔ Gatlinburg, TN (Great Smoky Mountains).
✔ Joshua Tree, CA (desert retreats).

💡 Lesson: The higher the demand, the more profitable (and tax-efficient) your rental will be.

◼ Step 2: Use Cost Segregation & Bonus Depreciation

Once you own a short-term rental, use a cost segregation study to accelerate depreciation deductions.

📌 Example: How Cost Segregation Saves $50,000 in Taxes

- You buy an STR for $600,000.
- A cost segregation study finds that $200,000 qualifies for bonus depreciation.
- Instead of waiting 27.5 years, you deduct $200,000 in Year 1.
- If you're in the 35% tax bracket, that's an immediate $70,000 tax savings.

💡 Lesson: The STR loophole + bonus depreciation = huge tax-free income.

⬛ Step 3: Self-Manage Your STR (Or Work More Than Your Property Manager)

To qualify for STR tax benefits, you must materially participate—which means you must be involved in managing the property.

📌 Ways to Prove Material Participation:
✔ Handling guest check-ins and check-outs.
✔ Coordinating cleanings and maintenance.
✔ Responding to guest messages and reviews.
✔ Marketing and pricing adjustments.
✔ Managing booking platforms (Airbnb, VRBO).

💡 Lesson: If you spend at least 100 hours AND more than anyone else, you qualify for STR tax benefits.

⬛ Step 4: Combine the STR Loophole with The Buy, Borrow, Die Strategy

📌 Step 1: Buy a Short-Term Rental Using OPM → Use low-down-payment loans (FHA, DSCR, or 10% down second-home loans).
📌 Step 2: Rent It for 7 Days or Less on Average → Qualify as an active business.
📌 Step 3: Use Bonus Depreciation to Deduct 100% of Certain Costs → Take huge tax deductions upfront.
📌 Step 4: Offset W-2 or Business Income with STR Tax Deductions → Reduce taxable income by tens of thousands of dollars.
📌 Step 5: Refinance Instead of Selling → Take out cash tax-free without triggering capital gains.
📌 Step 6: Pass the Property to Heirs Tax-Free → Use a stepped-up cost basis to eliminate taxes for your heirs.

💡 Lesson: STR owners can legally wipe out taxes while building long-term wealth.

Avoiding IRS Red Flags (How to Stay Audit-Proof)

Because this loophole is so powerful, the IRS scrutinizes STR claims.

📌 **Best Practices to Stay Compliant:**
✔ Track all hours spent managing your STR (use a spreadsheet or time-tracking app).
✔ Keep guest booking records (Airbnb and VRBO reports).
✔ Document communication with guests, cleaners, and maintenance teams.
✔ If using cost segregation, work with a tax professional.

💡 Lesson: The STR loophole is 100% legal, but documentation is key to protecting your tax savings.

32

House Hacking

Transforming Your Home from Liability to Tax-Free Asset

Most people think of their home as a place to live, but what if I told you it could also be a cash-flowing asset that builds wealth while you live for free?

That's exactly what House Hacking allows you to do.

This strategy turns your primary residence into an income-generating, tax-efficient investment—helping you build wealth faster while reducing or eliminating your housing costs.

In this chapter, I'll show you:
- How house hacking allows you to live for free (or even make money).
- The best ways to house hack (even if you don't want roommates).
- How to use tax deductions to maximize house hacking benefits.

What Is House Hacking?

House hacking is a real estate strategy where you live in one part of a property while renting out the other units or rooms to offset your mortgage.

📌 Why This Matters:
- Reduces (or eliminates) your housing costs.
- Allows you to build wealth through real estate while living in your home.
- Qualifies for massive tax deductions to lower taxable income.

💡 Lesson: Instead of paying a mortgage every month, house hacking lets someone else pay it for you.

How Much Can You Save with House Hacking?

📌 Example: Living for Free with House Hacking

- You buy a $500,000 duplex with an FHA loan (3.5% down = $17,500).
- Your monthly mortgage payment = $3,200.
- You rent the other unit for $2,500/month.
- Your total housing cost drops to just $700/month instead of $3,200.

📌 Example: Making Money While Living for Free

- You buy a $400,000 single-family home with a finished basement.
- You rent out the basement on Airbnb for $2,000/month.
- Your mortgage is $2,000/month → Your Airbnb rental covers the entire payment.
- You live in the house for free while making $500/month in profit.

💡 Lesson: House hacking lets you own property, build wealth, and reduce or eliminate your housing costs.

Best House Hacking Strategies

◼ 1. Buy a Duplex, Triplex, or Fourplex (Multi-Unit House Hacking)

📌 How It Works:

- You live in one unit and rent out the others.
- The rental income covers your mortgage and expenses.
- You get the benefits of homeownership while building wealth.

✔ Best For: First-time buyers, FHA loan users, long-term real estate investors.

💡 Example: A fourplex generates $8,000/month in rent → Your mortgage is $5,500/month → You live for free + make $2,500 in cash flow!

◼ 2. Rent Out Extra Bedrooms (Roommate House Hacking)

📌 How It Works:

- You buy a house and rent out extra bedrooms to roommates.
- Each roommate pays a portion of the mortgage.
- Works well in high-demand rental markets (college towns, cities).

✔ Best For: People who don't mind sharing space and want to save money fast.

💡 Example: Buy a 3-bedroom home for $350,000 → Rent out 2 bedrooms at $1,200 each → Your mortgage is covered, and you live for free.

🟫 3. Airbnb a Spare Room or In-Law Suite (Short-Term Rental House Hacking)

📌 How It Works:

- Instead of renting long-term, you list an extra room, basement, or guesthouse on Airbnb.
- Short-term rentals often earn 2-3x more than long-term tenants.

✔ Best For: People who live in tourist-friendly cities or near major events.

💡 Example: You rent a spare room for $100 per night on Airbnb. If booked 20 nights per month, you make $2,000/month—covering your entire mortgage.

🟫 4. Rent Out a Garage, Shed, or Driveway (Non-Traditional House Hacking)

📌 How It Works:

- Rent out storage space, garages, or parking spots.
- Services like Neighbor.com let you rent extra space without having tenants inside your house.

✔ Best For: Homeowners in urban areas with limited parking or extra storage space.

💡 Example: Rent out your driveway for $300/month + garage for $500/month → That's $800/month in passive income with zero tenant hassles.

Best Loans for House Hacking

The best way to house hack is to use low-down-payment loans to buy a property with as little cash as possible.

📌 **Top House Hacking Loan Options:**

Loan Type	Down Payment	Best For
FHA Loan	3.5%	First-time buyers, multi-unit house hackers
VA Loan	0%	Veterans and active military
Conventional (Owner-Occupied)	3-5%	Primary residence buyers
USDA Loan	0%	Rural homebuyers

💡 Lesson: With an FHA loan, you can buy a duplex, triplex, or fourplex with just 3.5% down—making house hacking even more affordable.

House Hacking Tax Benefits

House hacking doesn't just reduce your housing costs—it also comes with major tax benefits.

📌 **Key Tax Deductions for House Hackers:**
◼ **Mortgage Interest Deduction** → Reduce taxable income with interest write-offs.
◼ **Depreciation** → Write off a portion of your rental space over 27.5 years.
◼ **Home Office Deduction** → If you work from home, claim tax-free space.
◼ **Repairs & Maintenance** → Deduct expenses related to the rental portion of your home.
◼ **Property Taxes** → Deduct a portion of property taxes on the rental space.

💡 Lesson: Renting part of your home lets you legally reduce taxable income while keeping rental profits tax-free.

How House Hacking Fits Into the Buy, Borrow, Die Strategy

📌 **Step 1: Buy a Multi-Unit Property with an FHA or VA Loan** → Low down payment, easy entry.
📌 **Step 2: Rent Out Extra Units or Rooms** → Reduce or eliminate mortgage payments.

📌 Step 3: Use Rental Income to Pay Down the Mortgage → Build equity faster.
📌 Step 4: Refinance and Pull Out Tax-Free Cash → Use equity to buy more properties.
📌 Step 5: Pass the Property to Heirs Tax-Free → Stepped-up cost basis eliminates capital gains taxes.

💡 Lesson: House hacking is the fastest way to start real estate investing while paying little to no housing costs.

PART THREE

Income and Asset Protection

The third Pillar of a Buy, Borrow, Die strategy

33

Maximizing the Benefits of Term Life Insurance

Protecting Wealth with Smart Riders

Life insurance isn't just about protecting your family when you're gone—it's also a powerful tool for **wealth preservation, tax-free inheritance, and even strategic investing.**

Most people overlook **term life insurance** because they think it's only useful if they pass away early. But the **wealthy use term life strategically**—not just for protection, but also to **maximize financial flexibility, secure assets, and reduce tax burdens.**

In this chapter, I'll show you:
■ Why term life insurance is an essential part of a Buy, Borrow, Die strategy.
■ The best riders to add for financial security and investment advantages.
■ How to structure term life insurance to protect your assets and heirs.

Why Term Life Insurance?

Unlike **whole life insurance**, which builds cash value (but comes with high fees), **term life insurance** is designed to provide **pure protection at the lowest possible cost.**

📌 Why This Matters:
■ **It's affordable** – Term life is **10-20x cheaper** than whole life.
■ **It provides high coverage for a low cost** – You can get a **$1 million policy for $50/month.**
■ **It protects your assets and heirs** – Ensures debts and taxes don't wipe out your estate.
■ **It can be structured with smart riders** – Adding key benefits for financial security.

💡 **Lesson:** Term life insurance isn't just about death—it's about financial **security, legacy planning, and risk management.**

How Term Life Insurance Fits Into Buy, Borrow, Die

Wealthy individuals use life insurance as a **critical part of their financial strategy.**

📌 **Here's how term life supports Buy, Borrow, Die:**
✔ **Buy** → Protect real estate, investments, and assets from financial risks.
✔ **Borrow** → Ensure debt is covered in case of unexpected death.
✔ **Die** → Pass wealth tax-free to heirs with proper planning.

💡 **Lesson:** The right term life insurance **protects your family and assets while keeping your wealth intact.**

Best Term Life Insurance Riders to Maximize Protection

A basic term life policy provides **a lump sum payout** upon death. But adding the **right riders** can turn a simple policy into a **powerful financial tool.**

📌 **Top Term Life Insurance Riders for Wealth Protection:**

Rider	What It Does	Why It's Useful
Return of Premium (ROP)	Refunds all premiums paid if you outlive the policy.	Provides a built-in savings component.
Accelerated Death Benefit	Lets you access part of your death benefit if diagnosed with a terminal illness.	Helps cover medical expenses without liquidating assets.
Waiver of Premium	Waives premiums if you become disabled.	Keeps your coverage active even if you can't work.
Conversion Option	Allows you to convert term life into permanent life insurance.	Provides long-term flexibility.
Critical Illness Rider	Pays out a portion of the policy if you suffer a serious illness.	Helps with unexpected medical costs without draining savings.

💡 **Lesson:** Adding the right riders **enhances term life insurance**, making it a **flexible financial asset** instead of just a death benefit.

How to Use Term Life Insurance to Protect Your Real Estate & Investments

If you have **rental properties, mortgages, or investment debt**, term life insurance can act as a **safety net**, ensuring your assets remain protected.

📌 **Example: Protecting Your Investment Properties**

- You own **$2 million in rental properties** with **$1.5 million in mortgages**.
- A **$2 million term life insurance policy** ensures your heirs **inherit the properties debt-free.**
- If you pass away unexpectedly, the **insurance payout clears the debt—preventing forced sales or foreclosure.**

💡 **Lesson:** Term life insurance ensures that **your real estate empire survives beyond you.**

How to Structure Term Life Insurance for Tax-Free Wealth Transfer

Unlike stocks, real estate, or retirement accounts, **life insurance payouts are 100% tax-free.**

📌 **Strategies to Maximize Tax-Free Wealth Transfer:**
✔ **Name your heirs as beneficiaries** → Avoid probate and pass wealth directly.
✔ **Use an Irrevocable Life Insurance Trust (ILIT)** → Keep the payout outside your taxable estate.
✔ **Pair with a Roth IRA or real estate assets** → Create multiple layers of tax-free inheritance.
✔ **Use life insurance to pay estate taxes** → Protect generational wealth from IRS claims.

💡 **Lesson:** Life insurance is one of the **only assets that passes to heirs completely tax-free.**

How to Get the Best Term Life Insurance Policy

📌 **Step 1: Determine Your Coverage Needs**
✔ Multiply your **annual income by 10-15x** (e.g., if you make $100K, get a $1M-$1.5M policy).
✔ Add coverage for any **outstanding debts (mortgages, loans, business obligations).**

📌 **Step 2: Choose the Right Term Length**
✔ **20-30 years** → Ideal for long-term protection.
✔ **10-15 years** → Best for short-term financial security.

📌 **Step 3: Compare Multiple Providers**
✔ **Best for affordability:** Haven Life, Banner Life, AIG.
✔ **Best for high coverage:** Protective Life, Prudential.
✔ **Best for conversion options:** MassMutual, Northwestern Mutual.

📌 **Step 4: Get a Medical Exam (or No-Exam Policy)**
✔ **Fully underwritten policies** offer the **lowest rates**.
✔ **No-exam policies** are convenient but cost **10-30% more**.

💡 **Lesson:** The best policy is **one that provides high coverage at the lowest cost with flexible options.**

How Term Life Insurance Fits Into the Buy, Borrow, Die Strategy

📌 **Step 1: Buy a Term Life Insurance Policy** → Protect real estate, assets, and investments.
📌 **Step 2: Use Riders to Enhance Protection** → Add **return of premium, disability waiver, and accelerated benefits.**
📌 **Step 3: Use an ILIT to Pass Wealth Tax-Free** → Keep the **payout outside of your taxable estate.**
📌 **Step 4: Cover Mortgages & Business Debt** → Ensure your heirs **inherit properties without financial burden.**
📌 **Step 5: Use the Death Benefit for Estate Liquidity** → Avoid **forced asset sales and protect generational wealth.**

💡 **Lesson:** The right term life insurance strategy **ensures that your assets are protected and your heirs receive wealth tax-free.**

34

Indexed Universal Life Insurance

The Swiss Army Knife of Investing and Tax Avoidance

Most people think of life insurance as just a safety net—a way to ensure their family gets a payout when they pass away. But the wealthy don't just use life insurance for protection.

They use Indexed Universal Life Insurance (IUL) as a powerful wealth-building tool that provides tax-free growth, retirement income, and estate planning benefits—all in one flexible package.

What Makes IUL a Swiss Army Knife?

■ Tax-Free Growth → Your money grows tax-deferred like a Roth IRA.
■ Tax-Free Withdrawals → You can access your cash without paying income tax.
■ Market-Linked Returns (Without Risk of Loss) → Earn stock market-like returns with no risk of losing money.
■ Permanent Life Insurance Coverage → Provides lifelong financial security.

In this chapter, I'll show you:
✔ How IUL works and why wealthy people use it.
✔ How to use IUL to build wealth while avoiding taxes.
✔ The right way to structure an IUL policy to maximize benefits.

What Is Indexed Universal Life Insurance (IUL)?

IUL is a type of permanent life insurance that combines:
✔ A tax-free investment account (cash value that grows over time).
✔ A life insurance death benefit (paid out to your heirs tax-free).

Unlike whole life insurance (which has fixed, low returns), IUL lets you earn stock market-like returns without market risk.

📌 **How It Works:**
✔ You pay premiums → Part of the money funds your life insurance.
✔ The rest goes into a cash value account → This account grows based on stock market performance.
✔ You can access your cash tax-free → Through policy loans and withdrawals.

💡 **Lesson:** IUL is NOT just life insurance—it's a tax-free investment vehicle with powerful financial benefits.

How IUL Works as an Investment (Without Market Risk)

One of the biggest misconceptions about IUL is that it's like investing directly in the stock market.

📌 **Here's the truth:**
✔ Your cash value is linked to an index (S&P 500, Nasdaq, etc.).
✔ You earn a percentage of the market's gains (usually capped at 10-12%).
✔ If the market crashes, you don't lose money (your returns are never negative).

📌 **Example: How IUL Protects Your Money**

Year	S&P 500 Return	Your IUL Return (with 12% Cap, 0% Floor)
Year 1	+15%	+12% (capped at 12%)
Year 2	-25%	0% (your money is protected)
Year 3	+8%	+8%

💡 **Lesson:** IUL lets you earn stock market-like returns without ever losing money.

How IUL Fits Into the Buy, Borrow, Die Strategy

The wealthy use IUL because it aligns perfectly with the Buy, Borrow, Die strategy.

📌 **Here's how:**
✔ Buy → Use IUL as a tax-free wealth-building tool.
✔ Borrow → Take tax-free loans against the cash value for retirement or investing.
✔ Die → Pass wealth to heirs tax-free with no probate or estate taxes.

💡 **Lesson:** IUL lets you accumulate tax-free wealth, borrow against it, and pass it on tax-free—just like real estate.

Why the Wealthy Use IUL (and Why You Should Too)

1. Tax-Free Growth (Better Than a 401(k) or IRA)

- 401(k) and traditional IRA withdrawals are taxed as income.
- Roth IRAs have contribution limits and income restrictions.
- IUL has no contribution limits and grows tax-free—like a supercharged Roth IRA.

📌 Example: How IUL Beats a 401(k)

- You contribute $10,000 per year to an IUL and a 401(k).
- After 30 years, both accounts grow to $1,000,000.
- 401(k) withdrawals are taxed at 30% → You only keep $700,000.
- IUL withdrawals are tax-free → You keep the full $1,000,000.

💡 Lesson: IUL eliminates future tax bills—unlike traditional retirement accounts.

2. Tax-Free Withdrawals & Loans (Retirement Income Without Taxes)

- You can borrow against your cash value tax-free (unlike a 401(k) or IRA).
- No required minimum distributions (RMDs).
- No penalties for early withdrawals.

📌 Example: Tax-Free Retirement Income with IUL

- At age 60, you have $1 million in IUL cash value.
- You take out $50,000 per year in policy loans (tax-free).
- Unlike a 401(k), you owe zero income tax.

💡 Lesson: IUL lets you retire with tax-free income—keeping more of your money.

3. Lifetime Protection (Unlike Term Life Insurance, IUL Never Expires)

- Term life insurance expires after 20-30 years.
- IUL lasts for life—ensuring your heirs get a tax-free death benefit.

📌 Why It Matters:
✔ You always have coverage, no matter how long you live.
✔ Your cash value continues growing tax-free.
✔ Your family receives a guaranteed payout.

💡 Lesson: IUL provides permanent financial security—unlike term life insurance.

4. Estate Planning & Wealth Transfer (Tax-Free Inheritance)

- Life insurance is one of the only assets that transfers 100% tax-free.
- No estate taxes, no probate, no delays.

📌 Example: How IUL Passes Wealth Tax-Free

- John has $5 million in real estate & investments.
- He also has a $2 million IUL policy.
- When he dies, his heirs inherit the $2 million tax-free, covering estate taxes.

💡 Lesson: IUL ensures your wealth is protected and transferred tax-free to the next generation.

How to Structure an IUL Policy for Maximum Benefits

Not all IUL policies are created equal. To maximize benefits, you need to structure it properly.

📌 How to Set Up Your IUL the Right Way:
✔ Max Fund the Policy → Pay as much as possible into the cash value (without violating IRS rules).
✔ Use the Lowest Death Benefit Allowed → This ensures more money goes into your cash value, not insurance fees.
✔ Choose the Best Indexing Strategy → S&P 500, Nasdaq, or international indexes for maximum growth.
✔ Add a Long-Term Care (LTC) Rider → Allows you to use your death benefit while you're still alive if needed.

💡 Lesson: Properly structuring your IUL ensures maximum tax-free growth and retirement income.

PART FOUR

Cryptocurrency

The Fourth Pillar of a Buy, Borrow, Die strategy

35

Bitcoin vs Bucks

Why Digital Coins Beat the Unlimited Dollar Machine

For decades, the U.S. dollar has been the backbone of the global financial system. But in recent years, a **new contender has emerged**—one that **isn't controlled by governments, can't be printed at will, and offers a decentralized way to store and grow wealth: Bitcoin.**

Bitcoin isn't just a currency—it's a **revolution against the unlimited printing of dollars.** While traditional money (**fiat currency**) loses value due to inflation and government policies, Bitcoin is designed to be **scarce, secure, and resistant to manipulation.**

In this chapter, I'll show you:
■ **Why fiat currency loses value over time (and why Bitcoin doesn't).**
■ **How Bitcoin protects your wealth against inflation.**
■ **Why digital money is the future of financial freedom.**

Why the U.S. Dollar Is Losing Value

The U.S. government controls the dollar, and **whenever it needs more money, it prints it.**

📌 **Since 2020 alone, over $5 trillion has been printed**—causing massive inflation.

📌 **What happens when the money supply increases?**
✔ **Prices go up** (your money buys less).
✔ **Your savings lose value over time.**
✔ **The cost of living rises faster than wages.**

📌 **Example: How the Dollar Has Lost Value Over Time**

- In **1971**, a loaf of bread cost **$0.25**.
- In **2024**, the same loaf costs $4-$5.
- The dollar has lost over **90% of its purchasing power in the last 50 years.**

💡 **Lesson:** Fiat money always loses value over time because governments can print unlimited amounts of it.

Why Bitcoin Is Different: A Scarce Digital Asset

Bitcoin is the opposite of fiat money. **It's decentralized, limited in supply, and immune to inflation.**

📌 **Key Features That Make Bitcoin Unique:**
✔ **Fixed Supply (21 Million Coins Maximum)** → Unlike dollars, more Bitcoin can't be printed.
✔ **Decentralized** → No government or central bank controls Bitcoin.
✔ **Borderless & Global** → Can be used anywhere in the world, anytime.
✔ **Secure & Transparent** → Transactions are recorded on a public blockchain.

📌 **Example: Bitcoin vs. the U.S. Dollar**

Feature	Bitcoin	U.S. Dollar
Supply Limit?	Yes (21M max)	No (Unlimited printing)
Inflation-Proof?	Yes	No
Decentralized?	Yes	No (Government-controlled)
Can Be Censored?	No	Yes (Banks can freeze accounts)
Borderless?	Yes	No (Requires banks & SWIFT system)

💡 **Lesson:** Bitcoin is a **digital version of gold—scarce, decentralized, and resistant to inflation.**

Bitcoin as a Hedge Against Inflation

📌 **The More Money Governments Print, The More Valuable Bitcoin Becomes.**

Why?

✔ Fiat money loses value over time due to inflation.
✔ Bitcoin gains value over time due to scarcity.

📌 **Example: Bitcoin vs. Inflation Over the Last 10 Years**

- In **2013**, Bitcoin was worth **$100**.

163

- In **2024,** Bitcoin is worth **over $50,000.**
- Meanwhile, the U.S. dollar **has lost over 30% of its value** due to inflation.

💡 Lesson: Bitcoin's limited supply makes it a better store of value than fiat money.

Bitcoin vs. Gold: The Ultimate Store of Value?

Gold has been a **safe haven asset** for centuries, but Bitcoin is proving to be even better.

📌 Gold vs. Bitcoin: Which Is the Better Store of Value?

Feature	Gold	Bitcoin
Limited Supply?	Yes	Yes (21M max)
Easily Transportable?	No (Heavy & expensive to move)	Yes (Instant transactions worldwide)
Hard to Confiscate?	No (Governments can seize gold)	Yes (Private keys protect Bitcoin)
Divisible?	No (Hard to break into small units)	Yes (Can be divided into tiny fractions)

💡 Lesson: Bitcoin is **faster, more secure, and easier to store and transfer than gold.**

Bitcoin as a Global Financial System

Unlike banks and traditional financial institutions, Bitcoin **doesn't require approval from governments or corporations.**

📌 Why This Matters:
✔ **No middlemen** – You control your own money.
✔ **Accessible to anyone** – All you need is an internet connection.
✔ **No bank accounts required** – People in developing countries can store value securely.

📌 Example: Bitcoin Banking the Unbanked

- Over **1.7 billion people worldwide don't have bank accounts.**
- Bitcoin allows them to **store and transfer money without a bank.**
- Countries like **El Salvador** have made Bitcoin **legal tender** to help people without banking access.

💡 Lesson: Bitcoin is **a financial system for the entire world, not just the wealthy.**

How Bitcoin Fits Into the Buy, Borrow, Die Strategy

The wealthy **use assets like real estate, stocks, and Bitcoin to accumulate wealth without paying taxes.**

📌 **Here's how Bitcoin fits into the strategy:**
✔ **Buy Bitcoin** → Accumulate Bitcoin as a store of value (like digital gold).
✔ **Borrow Against It (Tax-Free)** → Use Bitcoin as collateral for tax-free loans (instead of selling and paying capital gains taxes).
✔ **Die & Pass It to Heirs Tax-Free** → Bitcoin can be passed to family members without government interference.

📌 **Example: Using Bitcoin for Tax-Free Wealth Growth**

- Instead of selling Bitcoin and paying **20-30% capital gains tax**,
- Wealthy investors **borrow against their Bitcoin tax-free.**
- They **use the borrowed money to buy assets like real estate or stocks.**

💡 **Lesson:** Bitcoin isn't just money—it's an **asset that can be leveraged for tax-free wealth building.**

36

Bitcoin ETFs

The Smart Way to Hold Digital Gold Without the Hassle

Bitcoin is often called "digital gold" because it provides a scarce, decentralized, and inflation-resistant store of value. However, buying and storing Bitcoin directly can be complicated—you need a digital wallet, private keys, and the technical know-how to protect your assets from hacks or loss.

For investors looking for an easier way to invest in Bitcoin, Bitcoin ETFs (Exchange-Traded Funds) provide a simple, secure, and hassle-free solution—allowing you to gain exposure to Bitcoin without dealing with digital wallets, exchanges, or private keys.

In this chapter, I'll show you:
◼ What a Bitcoin ETF is and how it works.
◼ The benefits of investing in Bitcoin ETFs instead of holding Bitcoin directly.
◼ How to use Bitcoin ETFs in your portfolio for long-term wealth building.

What Is a Bitcoin ETF?

A Bitcoin ETF (Exchange-Traded Fund) is a fund that tracks the price of Bitcoin and trades on traditional stock exchanges—just like regular ETFs that track stocks or commodities.

📌 **How It Works:**
✔ You buy shares of a Bitcoin ETF → Just like buying stock on the stock market.
✔ The ETF holds Bitcoin for you → You don't have to worry about security or storage.
✔ The ETF price follows Bitcoin's price movements → If Bitcoin's price goes up, the ETF value increases.

📌 **Example: How a Bitcoin ETF Works**

- If Bitcoin's price rises by 20%, the Bitcoin ETF also rises by approximately 20%.

- If Bitcoin's price drops by 10%, the ETF also falls by 10%.

💡 **Lesson:** Bitcoin ETFs allow any investor to gain exposure to Bitcoin without the complexity of direct ownership.

Why Bitcoin ETFs Are Better for Some Investors

While buying Bitcoin directly gives you full control, Bitcoin ETFs offer several advantages—especially for investors who want a simple, regulated way to invest in crypto.

📌 **Key Benefits of Bitcoin ETFs**

Feature	Bitcoin ETFs	Buying Bitcoin Directly
Ease of Purchase	✅ Buy through a stockbroker	❌ Requires a crypto exchange
No Private Keys Required	✅ ETF manages security for you	❌ You must secure your Bitcoin yourself
Regulated & Insured	✅ Government-regulated	❌ No consumer protections
Tax-Efficient Accounts	✅ Can be held in IRAs & 401(k)s	❌ Bitcoin itself doesn't qualify
Easier for Institutional Investors	✅ Can be included in hedge funds & retirement plans	❌ Many institutions can't hold direct crypto

💡 **Lesson:** Bitcoin ETFs are the easiest way for traditional investors to gain exposure to Bitcoin—without the risks of self-custody.

Types of Bitcoin ETFs: Spot vs. Futures ETFs

Not all Bitcoin ETFs are the same. There are two main types:

1. Spot Bitcoin ETFs (Best for Long-Term Investors)

✔ Directly holds real Bitcoin.
✔ Most closely tracks Bitcoin's price.
✔ Ideal for long-term investors who want true Bitcoin exposure.

📌 **Best Spot Bitcoin ETFs (2024):**

- Grayscale Bitcoin Trust (GBTC)
- iShares Bitcoin Trust (IBIT) – BlackRock

- Fidelity Wise Origin Bitcoin Trust (FBTC)

💡 Lesson: Spot Bitcoin ETFs are the closest thing to owning Bitcoin without managing it yourself.

2. Bitcoin Futures ETFs (Higher Risk, More Volatility)

✔ Holds Bitcoin futures contracts (not actual Bitcoin).
✔ Can experience price differences from real Bitcoin.
✔ Better for short-term trading but not ideal for long-term holding.

📌 Popular Bitcoin Futures ETFs:

- ProShares Bitcoin Strategy ETF (BITO)
- VanEck Bitcoin Strategy ETF (XBTF)

💡 Lesson: If you want real Bitcoin exposure, Spot Bitcoin ETFs are better than futures-based ETFs.

How Bitcoin ETFs Fit Into the Buy, Borrow, Die Strategy

Bitcoin ETFs provide an easy way to invest in Bitcoin while leveraging traditional financial tools.

📌 Here's how to use Bitcoin ETFs in the Buy, Borrow, Die strategy:

✔ Buy Bitcoin ETFs → Gain exposure to Bitcoin without dealing with private keys.
✔ Borrow Against Your Bitcoin ETFs Tax-Free → Use brokerage margin loans or portfolio lines of credit instead of selling and paying capital gains tax.
✔ Die & Pass Them to Heirs Tax-Free → Beneficiaries receive a stepped-up cost basis, eliminating capital gains taxes.

📌 Example: Using Bitcoin ETFs for Tax-Free Wealth Growth

- Instead of selling Bitcoin ETFs and paying 20-30% capital gains tax,
- Wealthy investors borrow against their ETF holdings tax-free.
- They use the borrowed money to buy more assets like real estate or stocks.

💡 Lesson: Bitcoin ETFs allow you to hold Bitcoin exposure in a traditional investment account while using tax-efficient borrowing strategies.

How to Invest in Bitcoin ETFs (Step-by-Step Guide)

Step 1: Open a Brokerage Account

- Choose a stock brokerage that offers Bitcoin ETFs (Fidelity, Schwab, TD Ameritrade, Robinhood, E-Trade, etc.).

Step 2: Decide How Much to Invest

- Start with 5-10% of your portfolio if you're new to Bitcoin.
- Consider dollar-cost averaging (buying regularly over time) instead of making a lump-sum purchase.

Step 3: Choose Between Spot and Futures ETFs

✔ Long-term investors → Spot Bitcoin ETFs (IBIT, FBTC, GBTC).
✔ Short-term traders → Bitcoin Futures ETFs (BITO, XBTF).

Step 4: Hold in a Tax-Advantaged Account (If Possible)

- Bitcoin ETFs can be held in retirement accounts (IRAs, Roth IRAs, 401(k)s).
- This allows tax-free or tax-deferred Bitcoin investing.

💡 Lesson: Bitcoin ETFs provide a hassle-free way to invest in Bitcoin through traditional brokerage accounts.

PART FIVE

Precious Metals

The Fifth Pillar of a Buy, Borrow, Die strategy

BUY
Buy assets (stocks & businesses)

BORROW
Loans to fund lifestyle expenses

DIE
Step up in assests to heirs

37

Golden Opportunities

Leveraging Buy, Borrow, Die to Acquire Gold and Precious Metals

Gold has been a **symbol of wealth for thousands of years**, and for good reason—it's a **hedge against inflation, a store of value, and a powerful asset to preserve wealth over generations.**

But what if I told you that the wealthy **don't just buy gold—they leverage it using the Buy, Borrow, Die strategy to grow their wealth while keeping their tax bill at zero?**

In this chapter, you'll learn:

■ Why gold and precious metals are essential for financial security.
■ How to acquire gold using Buy, Borrow, Die.
■ The best ways to store and invest in gold while avoiding taxes.

Why Gold and Precious Metals?

Gold isn't just a shiny rock—it's one of the **most powerful wealth-preservation tools** available.

📌 **Why Gold Is Important for Investors:**
✔ **Inflation Hedge** → Unlike cash, gold doesn't lose value when governments print money.
✔ **Crisis Protection** → Gold retains value during financial crashes, wars, and recessions.
✔ **Limited Supply** → Unlike fiat money, gold can't be printed or inflated away.
✔ **Tax-Free Wealth Transfer** → Physical gold can be passed to heirs with minimal taxation.

📌 **Example: Gold vs. U.S. Dollar Over Time**

- **1971:** Gold was **$35 per ounce.**
- **2024:** Gold is **over $2,000 per ounce.**

- Meanwhile, the U.S. dollar **has lost over 90% of its purchasing power.**

💡 Lesson: Gold is a **long-term store of value that protects wealth from inflation and economic instability.**

How the Wealthy Use Buy, Borrow, Die to Acquire Gold

The rich **don't just buy gold—they leverage it** to acquire more wealth while avoiding taxes.

📌 **Here's how they do it:**

✔ **Buy Gold** → Accumulate gold through **physical purchases, ETFs, or gold-backed IRAs.**
✔ **Borrow Against Gold (Tax-Free Loans)** → Instead of selling and triggering capital gains taxes, they use gold as collateral for tax-free loans.
✔ **Die & Pass Gold to Heirs Tax-Free** → Gold **can be inherited with a stepped-up cost basis**, eliminating capital gains taxes.

📌 **Example: Using Gold as Collateral for Tax-Free Borrowing**

- Sarah owns **$500,000 in physical gold**.
- Instead of selling it and paying **capital gains tax**, she takes out a **tax-free loan** using her gold as collateral.
- She uses the loan to **buy real estate, stocks, or more gold—without triggering taxes.**

💡 Lesson: The wealthy use gold as an asset to secure tax-free loans—allowing them to reinvest while keeping their gold holdings intact.

Best Ways to Acquire Gold (Without Getting Scammed)

There are **several ways to invest in gold**, but not all of them are created equal.

📌 **Best Ways to Own Gold & Precious Metals:**

1. Physical Gold (Best for Long-Term Security & Crisis Protection)

✔ **Gold bars & coins** → Ideal for storing wealth outside the banking system.
✔ **Where to buy:** Reputable dealers like **APMEX, JM Bullion, and Kitco.**
✔ **Storage options:** Home safes, bank vaults, or private depositories (**Brink's, Delaware Depository**).

📌 **Pros:**
✔ No counterparty risk (you own it outright).
✔ Can be passed to heirs tax-free.
✔ Provides direct control over your wealth.

📌 **Cons:**
✘ Requires secure storage.
✘ Can't be easily used for tax-free borrowing (unless stored with a custodian).

💡 **Lesson: Physical gold is the best hedge against financial collapse but requires proper security and storage.**

2. Gold ETFs & Gold Stocks (Best for Convenience & Liquidity)

✔ **Gold ETFs** → Track the price of gold without needing to store it.
✔ **Best ETFs:**

- SPDR Gold Shares (**GLD**)
- iShares Gold Trust (**IAU**)

✔ **Gold Mining Stocks** → Invest in companies that mine gold for leveraged exposure.
✔ **Best Gold Mining Stocks:**

- Newmont Corporation (**NEM**)
- Barrick Gold (**GOLD**)

📌 **Pros:**
✔ Easy to buy and sell like stocks.
✔ No need to worry about storage.
✔ Can be used in retirement accounts (IRAs, 401(k)s).

📌 **Cons:**
✘ Not as safe as physical gold (subject to financial system risks).
✘ No direct ownership of the metal.

💡 **Lesson:** Gold ETFs and mining stocks are **great for traders and investors who want exposure without dealing with physical storage.**

3. Gold-Backed IRAs (Best for Tax-Advantaged Investing)

✔ **Gold IRAs** → A self-directed IRA that lets you invest in **physical gold and silver** while getting tax advantages.
✔ **Where to open a Gold IRA:** Augusta Precious Metals, Goldco, Birch Gold Group.

📌 **Pros:**
✔ Gains grow **tax-free or tax-deferred**.
✔ IRS-approved custodians handle **secure storage**.
✔ Allows **diversification inside a retirement account**.

📌 **Cons:**
✘ You don't take physical possession of the gold.
✘ Withdrawals before retirement age **incur penalties**.

💡 **Lesson:** Gold IRAs are an excellent way to hold gold while enjoying tax benefits—but require a long-term mindset.

How to Use Gold for Tax-Free Wealth Transfer

Gold is one of the **best assets to pass to heirs** because it can avoid many of the taxes associated with cash, stocks, or real estate.

📌 **How to Pass Gold to Heirs Tax-Free:**
✔ **Gift gold gradually** → Stay under the annual gift tax limit (**$17,000 per recipient in 2024**).
✔ **Use a trust** → A **Gold Trust** can help avoid estate taxes.
✔ **Pass physical gold privately** → Unlike stocks, gold doesn't have to go through banks or probate courts.

📌 **Example: Passing Gold to the Next Generation Without Taxes**

- Mark owns **$1 million in gold**.
- Instead of selling it and triggering **capital gains tax**, he gradually gifts **$17,000 worth of gold per year** to his children.
- When he passes, his remaining gold is **inherited with a stepped-up cost basis—eliminating capital gains taxes.**

💡 **Lesson:** Gold allows for **quiet, tax-efficient wealth transfer without the interference of banks or the government.**

How to Store Gold Securely (Without Losing It to Theft or Confiscation)

📌 **Best Places to Store Gold Safely:**
✔ **Private Home Safes** → Ideal for smaller amounts (**Make sure it's fireproof & hidden!**).
✔ **Bank Safe Deposit Boxes** → Secure but not insured by the FDIC.
✔ **Private Gold Vaults (Best for Large Holdings)** → Brink's, Loomis, Delaware Depository.

📌 **Worst Places to Store Gold:**
✘ **Hiding it under your mattress** → Too easy to lose or steal.
✘ **Storing it in a foreign country without legal protections** → Risk of confiscation or inaccessibility.

💡 **Lesson: Proper storage is just as important as owning gold—never keep all your holdings in one place.**

PART SIX

Business Ownership

The solid Foundation of a Buy, Borrow, Die strategy

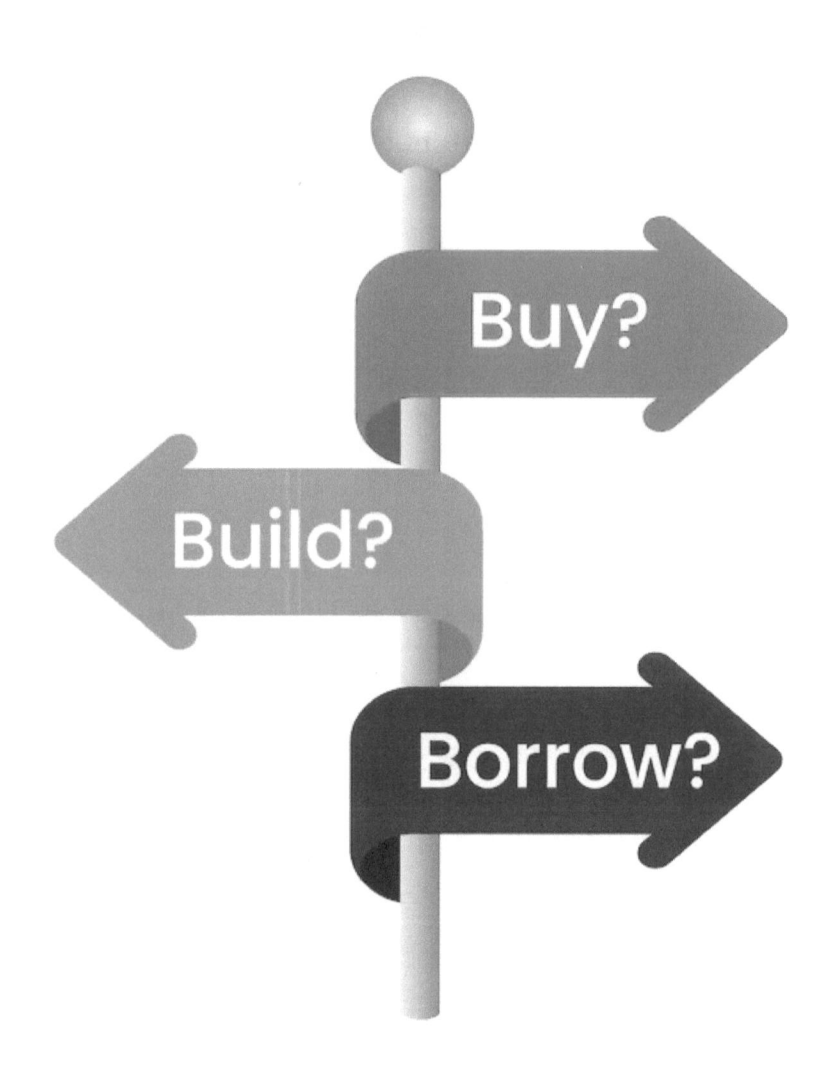

38

Tacos, Tequila, and Tax Breaks

Maximizing Your Business Deductions

If you're running a business, you're sitting on a **goldmine of tax deductions** that can legally lower your tax bill—sometimes to zero. The wealthy and financially savvy don't just make money; they **maximize every legal tax break available to keep more of it.**

And here's the best part: **Every meal, every trip, even the drinks you enjoy while discussing business—can all become tax-deductible.**

This chapter will show you:
- **How to turn everyday expenses into legal tax deductions.**
- **How to use meals, travel, and entertainment to lower your tax bill.**
- **How business owners (big and small) take full advantage of the tax code.**

The IRS Loves Business Owners More Than Employees

The tax code is written to benefit **business owners and investors—not W-2 employees.**

📌 **Why?**
✔ **Employees** pay taxes **before** they spend money.
✔ **Business owners** spend money first and pay taxes on what's left.

📌 **Example: Employee vs. Business Owner Taxation**

- John (W-2 Employee) earns **$100,000** and pays **30% in taxes ($30,000)** → He only keeps **$70,000**.
- Mike (Business Owner) earns **$100,000**, but first deducts **$40,000 in business expenses** → He's only taxed on **$60,000, saving $12,000 in taxes.**

💡 **Lesson:** If you're not using business deductions, you're **giving the IRS free money.**

How to Make Everyday Expenses Tax-Deductible

The key to maximizing tax savings is **turning ordinary expenses into business expenses.**

📌 **Top Business Tax Deductions You Should Be Taking:**

Expense	How to Deduct It
Meals & Drinks	Business meals (client meetings, team lunches) are **50% deductible**
Travel & Lodging	Flights, hotels, and rental cars for business travel are **100% deductible**
Home Office	If you work from home, a portion of your rent/mortgage, utilities, and internet is deductible
Car & Mileage	If you use your car for business, you can deduct mileage (**$0.67 per mile in 2024**) or actual expenses
Education & Training	Courses, books, and conferences to improve your business are **100% deductible**
Entertainment (Yes, Even Tequila!)	Taking clients out for drinks or events can be **50% deductible**
Marketing & Advertising	Facebook ads, Google ads, website costs, and business cards are **fully deductible**

💡 **Lesson:** Almost everything you do for your business can be **turned into a tax deduction.**

How to Write Off Business Meals (The Right Way)

1. Business Meals (50% Deductible)

- Must be **with a client, employee, or business partner.**
- Must discuss business **before, during, or after the meal.**
- Keep **receipts and notes on who you met** with & what was discussed.

📌 **Example: Writing Off Tacos & Tequila the Right Way**

- You take a **client to lunch at a Mexican restaurant** and discuss a business deal.
- The meal costs **$100**, and you deduct **$50 on your taxes (50% rule).**
- Over the year, if you spend $5,000 **on business meals, you reduce your taxable income by $2,500.**

💡 **Lesson:** If you're meeting with clients, vendors, or employees, **your meals should be tax-deductible.**

178

How to Write Off Business Travel (100% Deductible)

2. Business Travel (100% Deductible)

To qualify, your trip must be **primarily for business** (but you can still have fun).

📌 **What's Deductible on a Business Trip?**
✔ **Flights & Baggage Fees** → Fully deductible.
✔ **Hotels & Airbnb Stays** → Must be for business purposes.
✔ **Rental Cars & Uber** → Used for business meetings or events.
✔ **Meals & Entertainment** → 50% deductible if you're discussing business.
✔ **Conference Fees & Networking Events** → Fully deductible.

📌 Example: Turning a Trip into a Tax Deduction

- You attend a **business conference in Las Vegas**.
- You stay **4 nights in a hotel** (**100% deductible**).
- You meet clients for dinner (**50% deductible**).
- You **sightsee in your free time (non-deductible, but the trip still counts as business)**.

💡 Lesson: If you travel **at least 51% for business**, the **entire trip can be a write-off.**

How to Write Off a Car for Business Use

3. Business Vehicles & Mileage

📌 **You can deduct business vehicle expenses in two ways:**

✔ **Standard Mileage Deduction** → In 2024, you can deduct **$0.67 per mile driven for business.**
✔ **Actual Expenses Method** → Deduct **gas, maintenance, insurance, lease payments, and depreciation.**

📌 Example: Using Your Car for Business

- You drive **10,000 miles for business in a year.**
- You deduct **$0.67 per mile** → **$6,700 in tax savings!**

💡 **Lesson:** If you drive for business, **track your mileage using an app like MileIQ or Everlance.**

How to Write Off a Home Office (Even If You Rent)

4. The Home Office Deduction

If you work from home, you can deduct a portion of your **rent, mortgage, utilities, and internet.**

📌 **How to Calculate the Deduction:**
✔ **Simplified Method** → $5 per square foot (max 300 sq ft = $1,500 deduction).
✔ **Detailed Method** → Deduct **a percentage of your home expenses** (home office size ÷ total home size).

📌 **Example: Saving $3,000 with the Home Office Deduction**

- Your home is **2,000 sq ft** and your office is **200 sq ft** (**10% of your home**).
- Your total home expenses (rent, utilities, internet) = **$30,000**.
- You can deduct **10% of that ($3,000) as a business expense.**

💡 **Lesson:** If you work from home, **this is one of the easiest ways to lower your taxable income.**

How to Use Business Deductions in the Buy, Borrow, Die Strategy

📌 **Step 1: Buy Business Assets Using Tax Deductions** → Deduct business meals, travel, and home office expenses to reduce taxable income.
📌 **Step 2: Borrow Against Business Profits** → Instead of taking taxable income, use a business line of credit for tax-free cash flow.
📌 **Step 3: Die & Pass Business Assets Tax-Free** → Set up trusts and estate plans to pass your business and assets without excessive taxes.

📌 **Example: Using Business Deductions to Pay Less in Taxes**

- You earn **$200,000 in business income**.
- You deduct **$50,000 in business expenses**.
- You're only taxed on **$150,000 instead of $200,000**, saving **$15,000+ in taxes!**

💡 **Lesson: Business deductions let you legally lower your taxable income and keep more money in your pocket.**

39

S-Corp Secrets

How to Slash Your Taxes and Keep More of Your Money

If you own a business (or plan to start one), there's one powerful tax loophole that can help you legally reduce your tax bill, increase your take-home pay, and keep more of your hard-earned money—it's called the S-Corp Election.

The wealthy and financially savvy don't just work hard to make money—they structure their businesses strategically to keep more of it.

In this chapter, you'll learn:

- What an S-Corp is and how it saves you thousands in taxes.
- How to convert your business to an S-Corp and pay yourself tax-efficiently.
- The best way to use an S-Corp in the Buy, Borrow, Die strategy.

What Is an S-Corp and Why Does It Matter?

An S-Corporation (S-Corp) isn't a type of business—it's a tax election that allows business owners to avoid paying self-employment tax on a portion of their income.

📌 **Why This Matters:**
✔ Reduces payroll taxes (Social Security & Medicare).
✔ Allows business owners to take tax-free distributions.
✔ Separates personal and business income for better asset protection.

📌 **Example: The Difference Between an LLC and an S-Corp**

Business Structure	How You Pay Taxes
LLC (No S-Corp Election)	Pay **self-employment tax (15.3%)** on all profits
S-Corp	Pay yourself a **reasonable salary** and take **tax-free distributions** on remaining profits

💡 Lesson: An S-Corp is the best way to legally reduce your self-employment taxes while keeping your business profits.

How an S-Corp Saves You Thousands in Taxes

The Self-Employment Tax Problem (Why LLC Owners Overpay)

- If you operate as a sole proprietor or standard LLC, you pay 15.3% self-employment tax on ALL profits.
- This tax consists of Social Security (12.4%) and Medicare (2.9%).

📌 Example: Why LLC Owners Pay More Taxes

- You make $100,000 in business profit as an LLC.
- You owe $15,300 in self-employment tax, plus income tax on top of that.

💡 Lesson: If you don't elect S-Corp status, you're paying thousands in extra taxes.

How an S-Corp Reduces Taxes

- Instead of paying self-employment tax on all profits, you split your income into two parts:
  ✔ A "reasonable salary" → Pays payroll taxes (like a normal W-2 job).
  ✔ Tax-free distributions → The remaining business profits are NOT subject to self-employment tax.

📌 Example: How an S-Corp Saves $7,650 in Taxes

- You make $100,000 in business profit.
- You pay yourself a reasonable salary of $50,000 (which is subject to payroll taxes).
- The remaining $50,000 is taken as a tax-free distribution (no self-employment tax).
- Instead of paying $15,300 in self-employment tax, you only pay $7,650—saving you $7,650 in taxes!

💡 Lesson: By using an S-Corp, you legally avoid self-employment tax on part of your income—saving thousands per year.

How to Convert Your Business to an S-Corp (Step-by-Step Guide)

■ Step 1: Form an LLC (If You Haven't Already)

- If you don't have a business yet, start with an LLC (it provides liability protection).
- LLCs are flexible and easy to manage, but they pay full self-employment tax unless you elect S-Corp status.

■ Step 2: File IRS Form 2553 to Elect S-Corp Status

- Once your LLC is formed, file IRS Form 2553 to elect S-Corp status.
- This must be done within 75 days of starting your business (or by March 15 for an existing LLC).

📌 Pro Tip: If you miss the deadline, you can still request "relief for late election"—the IRS often grants it.

■ Step 3: Pay Yourself a "Reasonable Salary"

- The IRS requires S-Corp owners to pay themselves a reasonable salary before taking distributions.
- A "reasonable salary" depends on industry standards (typically 30-50% of profits).

📌 Example: How to Set a Reasonable Salary

- If your business makes $120,000 per year, a reasonable salary could be $40,000-$60,000.
- The rest ($60,000-$80,000) can be taken as tax-free distributions.

💡 Lesson: The lower your salary, the more you save on taxes—but it must be reasonable to avoid IRS scrutiny.

How an S-Corp Fits into the Buy, Borrow, Die Strategy

📌 Step 1: Use an S-Corp to Reduce Taxes

- Lower your self-employment tax burden by taking tax-free distributions.

- Deduct business expenses (travel, meals, home office, car).

📌 Step 2: Borrow Against Your Business Income Tax-Free

- Instead of paying yourself all at once (and triggering taxes),
- Use business credit lines and loans to access cash without selling assets.

📌 Step 3: Pass Your Business to Heirs Tax-Free

- Use trusts and estate planning to ensure your business assets transfer without estate taxes.
- Your heirs inherit the business at a stepped-up cost basis—eliminating capital gains taxes.

💡 Lesson: S-Corp status maximizes tax efficiency while allowing for tax-free borrowing and wealth transfer.

Common S-Corp Mistakes (and How to Avoid Them)

📌 Mistake #1: Not Paying Yourself a Salary

- The IRS requires S-Corp owners to pay themselves a reasonable salary.
- If you skip this step, the IRS can reclassify all earnings as salary and hit you with penalties.

📌 Mistake #2: Setting an Unrealistically Low Salary

- If your salary is too low, the IRS may audit your business and force you to pay back taxes.
- Keep it reasonable based on industry standards.

📌 Mistake #3: Not Keeping Clean Financial Records

- Use separate bank accounts for business and personal finances.
- Track all income, payroll, and business expenses to stay compliant.

💡 Lesson: If you follow the IRS rules, an S-Corp can save you thousands while keeping you audit-proof.

40

Turning Learning into Earning

Making Education a Business Expense

The wealthy don't just invest in stocks, real estate, or businesses—they invest in knowledge.

But here's the difference: They write off the cost of learning as a business expense—turning self-improvement into a tax-deductible investment.

The U.S. tax code allows business owners to deduct the cost of education, training, books, conferences, and coaching—if it helps them grow their business.

In this chapter, you'll learn:

■ How to make education expenses 100% tax-deductible.
■ What courses, books, and programs qualify for tax write-offs.
■ How to structure your learning expenses to maximize tax savings.

Why Education Should Be a Business Expense

Most people pay for education with after-tax dollars. But business owners and entrepreneurs can write off learning expenses as a business investment.

📌 Key Benefits of Making Education a Business Expense:
✔ Reduces taxable income → Lowers the amount you owe to the IRS.
✔ Helps grow your skills and business → A tax-free way to improve earning potential.
✔ Covers books, coaching, conferences, online courses, and more.

💡 Lesson: If your education helps you make more money in business, it can—and should—be a tax-deductible expense.

What Education Expenses Can You Deduct?

📌 The IRS allows you to deduct education expenses if they:
✔ Maintain or improve skills related to your business or job.
✔ Help you stay competitive in your industry.
✔ Are directly related to your business or profession.

📌 What You Can Write Off:

Category	Examples
Books & Industry Publications	Business books, trade magazines, professional journals
Online Courses & Webinars	Udemy, Coursera, LinkedIn Learning, niche business courses
Conferences & Seminars	Industry conferences, networking events, real estate seminars
Coaching & Consulting	Business coaching, mentorship programs, mastermind groups
Certifications & Licensing	CPA courses, real estate licensing, financial certifications
Tech & Skill Training	Coding bootcamps, marketing courses, AI & automation training

💡 Lesson: If a course, book, or event helps you improve your business or profession, it's 100% deductible.

How to Write Off Business Education (Step-by-Step Guide)

Step 1: Pay for Learning Through Your Business

- Use your business credit card or business bank account for all education-related purchases.
- This keeps records clean and separate from personal expenses.

Step 2: Track & Categorize Learning Expenses

- Use accounting software (QuickBooks, Xero) to log education expenses.
- Keep receipts, course confirmations, or proof of attendance.

Step 3: Deduct Learning Expenses on Your Tax Return

- If you're a sole proprietor or single-member LLC → Claim education expenses on Schedule C (Business Expenses).

- If you have an S-Corp or C-Corp → Deduct under "Employee Training & Education."

📌 Example: How to Save $5,000 in Taxes Using Education Deductions

- You spend $10,000 on business courses, coaching, and conferences.
- You're in the 25% tax bracket, meaning you save $2,500-$5,000 in taxes by deducting those expenses.

💡 Lesson: Education reduces taxable income, improves your business, and increases profits—all tax-free.

How to Turn Vacations into Business Education (Legally)

One of the biggest tax loopholes is combining travel with education.

📌 How to Make a Vacation a Tax-Deductible Business Trip:
✔ Attend a business conference in a vacation-friendly location (e.g., real estate seminar in Miami).
✔ Visit business-related sites (networking, factory tours, competitor analysis).
✔ Document business meetings and learning activities.

📌 Example: Turning a Trip to Mexico into a Business Deduction

- You travel to Cancún for a real estate conference (4 days).
- You stay an extra 3 days for leisure.
- Flights and hotel are 100% deductible because the primary purpose is business.
- Meals, transportation, and event fees are fully deductible.

💡 Lesson: If your trip is business-related, the IRS allows you to write off travel costs—while still enjoying your vacation.

How to Use Education Deductions in the Buy, Borrow, Die Strategy

📌 Step 1: Use Business Education to Improve Your Earning Potential → Learn high-income skills (marketing, sales, automation, real estate investing).
📌 Step 2: Deduct Learning Expenses to Reduce Taxes → Lower taxable income by writing off coaching, courses, and conferences.
📌 Step 3: Borrow Against Business Growth Tax-Free → Use increased income to take

loans against assets instead of withdrawing taxable income.

📌 Step 4: Pass Down Knowledge & Tax-Free Wealth → Teach heirs financial strategies and tax-saving techniques.

📌 Example: Using Business Learning to Build Tax-Free Wealth

- John is a real estate investor who spends $15,000 on seminars & coaching.
- He deducts those expenses from his taxable income, saving $5,000 in taxes.
- He uses the knowledge to acquire $1 million in new real estate.
- Instead of selling his properties, he borrows tax-free against them and reinvests.

💡 Lesson: Education isn't just knowledge—it's a tax-deductible tool for building real wealth.

Common Mistakes (And How to Avoid Them)

📌 Mistake #1: Not Paying for Education Through Your Business

- If you use personal accounts, you lose documentation and tax advantages.

📌 Mistake #2: Writing Off Education That's NOT Business-Related

- The IRS won't allow deductions for general education not related to your business or industry.
- Example: A doctor taking a real estate course probably can't deduct it—but a real estate investor can.

📌 Mistake #3: Not Keeping Receipts & Documentation

- Always save invoices, confirmation emails, and credit card statements.
- Use a business expense tracker to organize receipts.

💡 Lesson: If you follow IRS guidelines, education deductions are 100% legal and can save you thousands.

41

Section 179 Savings

Buy a Tesla for Your Business

What if I told you that you could buy a Tesla, write off most (or all) of it on your taxes, and drive it for nearly free—legally?

That's exactly what Section 179 of the IRS tax code allows business owners to do.

If your business needs a vehicle, you might as well make the IRS pay for it. The wealthy use this tax break to purchase luxury cars, SUVs, and trucks while slashing their tax bills.

In this chapter, you'll learn:

- How Section 179 allows you to deduct the full cost of a vehicle in the first year.
- Which vehicles qualify (including Teslas and other luxury cars).
- How to structure the purchase to maximize tax savings.

What Is Section 179 and How Does It Work?

Section 179 allows businesses to immediately deduct the full purchase price of qualifying equipment—including vehicles—rather than spreading the deduction over multiple years.

📌 **Key Benefits of Section 179:**
✔ Write off up to $28,900 (2024) for qualifying luxury cars.
✔ Write off up to 100% for SUVs, trucks, and vans over 6,000 lbs.
✔ Applies to new and used vehicles, as long as they're for business use.
✔ Can be combined with bonus depreciation for even more savings.

💡 **Lesson:** If you're buying a business vehicle, you can deduct thousands in taxes immediately.

How to Write Off a Tesla (Or Any Luxury Car) Using Section 179

Not all vehicles qualify for a 100% deduction, but Tesla and other luxury cars still qualify for large write-offs.

📌 Here's how the deduction works:

Vehicle Type	Max Write-Off (2024)
Luxury Sedans (Tesla Model 3, BMW, Mercedes, etc.)	Up to $28,900
SUVs & Trucks Over 6,000 lbs (Tesla Model X, Cybertruck, Range Rover, G-Wagon, Ford F-150, etc.)	Up to 100% of the purchase price

💡 Lesson: If you buy a Tesla Model X or Cybertruck, you can write off the entire purchase price.

What Are the Rules for Section 179?

To qualify, the vehicle must:
✔ Be used for business at least 50% of the time.
✔ Be purchased (or financed) and put into service by December 31 of the tax year.
✔ Be used by a business entity (LLC, S-Corp, or sole proprietor).

📌 Example: Writing Off a Tesla Model X with Section 179

- You buy a Tesla Model X for $100,000 for your business.
- Since the Model X weighs over 6,000 lbs, you qualify for 100% depreciation in Year 1.
- If you're in the 35% tax bracket, this saves you $35,000 in taxes.

💡 Lesson: If your business needs a vehicle, Section 179 can save you tens of thousands of dollars.

How to Use Business Financing to Buy a Tesla Tax-Free

You don't need to pay cash to take advantage of Section 179.

📌 How to Buy a Tesla with Zero Out-of-Pocket Cost:
✔ Step 1: Finance or Lease the Tesla Through Your Business.

✔ Step 2: Deduct the Full Amount Using Section 179.
✔ Step 3: Use Tax Savings to Cover Your Payments.

📌 Example: Buying a Tesla Model 3 with Business Financing

- You buy a Tesla Model 3 for $50,000 using a business auto loan.
- Section 179 allows you to write off $28,900 in Year 1.
- If you're in the 35% tax bracket, that's a $10,000 tax savings.
- You use the tax savings to cover most of your monthly payments.

💡 Lesson: The IRS lets you write off a car you haven't even fully paid for yet.

How to Use Your Tesla for Business (And Stay IRS-Compliant)

The IRS requires that the vehicle be used for business at least 50% of the time.

📌 Best Ways to Prove Business Use:
✔ Log miles using apps like MileIQ or Everlance.
✔ Use the Tesla for client meetings, business trips, and work-related errands.
✔ If you work from home, track miles from your home office.

💡 Lesson: Keep a record of business trips to ensure your deduction is audit-proof.

Combining Section 179 With Bonus Depreciation

For even bigger savings, you can combine Section 179 with bonus depreciation.

📌 What Is Bonus Depreciation?

- Allows 100% write-off on new & used vehicles over 6,000 lbs.
- Applies even if you exceed the Section 179 limit.
- Bonus depreciation is being phased out (drops to 80% in 2024 and 60% in 2025).

📌 Example: Buying a Range Rover with Bonus Depreciation

- You buy a Range Rover for $120,000 in 2024.
- Section 179 lets you deduct $28,900 immediately.
- Bonus depreciation lets you deduct the remaining $91,100 in Year 1.
- If you're in the 35% tax bracket, that's a $42,000 tax savings.

💡 Lesson: If you're buying a luxury SUV or truck over 6,000 lbs, 2024 is the best year to take full advantage of bonus depreciation.

How to Use Vehicle Tax Deductions in the Buy, Borrow, Die Strategy

📌 Step 1: Buy a Business Vehicle Using Section 179 → Deduct the full cost in Year 1.
📌 Step 2: Borrow Against Business Cash Flow → Instead of withdrawing taxable income, use loans against your business.
📌 Step 3: Pass Down Vehicles & Assets Tax-Free → Transfer vehicles through estate planning or trusts.

📌 Example: Using Section 179 to Cut Taxes & Reinvest

- Maria owns an LLC making $200,000 per year.
- She buys a Tesla Model X for $100,000 and writes off the full amount.
- Her taxable income drops to $100,000, saving $35,000 in taxes.
- She reinvests the tax savings into more business growth.

💡 Lesson: Section 179 helps you reduce taxes while reinvesting in your business.

Common Section 179 Mistakes (And How to Avoid Them)

📌 Mistake #1: Not Using the Car Enough for Business

- If business use falls below 50%, you may have to pay back part of the deduction.
- Solution: Track miles and business usage carefully.

📌 Mistake #2: Not Buying Before December 31

- The vehicle must be in service before the year ends to qualify.
- Solution: Buy and register the vehicle before December 31.

📌 Mistake #3: Not Using Bonus Depreciation

- If your vehicle costs more than $28,900, you may be leaving money on the table.
- Solution: Use bonus depreciation to maximize your deduction.

💡 Lesson: Follow IRS rules and track business use to maximize your Section 179 savings.

42

Tax-Savvy Health

How to Save on Taxes While Protecting Your Well-Being

Most people think of healthcare as one of their biggest expenses—but what if I told you that the wealthy turn healthcare costs into a tax-saving strategy?

By using tax-advantaged health accounts, strategic deductions, and smart business structures, you can reduce your taxable income, save thousands on medical expenses, and even invest tax-free for future healthcare needs.

In this chapter, you'll learn:

▪ How to deduct medical expenses legally and effectively.
▪ How to use Health Savings Accounts (HSAs) for tax-free medical investing.
▪ How business owners can pay for healthcare with pre-tax dollars.

How the Wealthy Use Healthcare to Reduce Taxes

Healthcare expenses can be deducted or paid for with tax-free money—but only if you know how to structure them properly.

📌 **The Three Best Tax-Saving Health Strategies:**
✔ Deduct medical expenses → Reduce your taxable income.
✔ Use tax-advantaged health accounts (HSAs, FSAs, HRAs) → Pay for healthcare tax-free.
✔ Set up a business health plan → Write off insurance premiums and medical costs.

💡 **Lesson:** If you're paying for medical expenses with after-tax dollars, you're overpaying.

Strategy #1: Deduct Medical Expenses on Your Taxes

Most people don't realize that medical expenses can be deducted—but only if they exceed 7.5% of your adjusted gross income (AGI).

📌 How It Works:
✔ You can deduct medical expenses that exceed 7.5% of your AGI.
✔ Qualifying expenses include doctor visits, prescriptions, surgeries, therapy, and even alternative treatments.

📌 Example: Deducting Medical Expenses to Lower Taxes

- John earns $100,000 per year.
- His medical expenses total $12,000 for the year.
- Since 7.5% of his AGI = $7,500, he can deduct the remaining $4,500 from his taxable income.

💡 Lesson: If you have high medical expenses, you can use deductions to lower your tax bill.

Strategy #2: Use a Health Savings Account (HSA) for Tax-Free Healthcare Investing

An HSA (Health Savings Account) is one of the most powerful tax-free investment vehicles available—but most people don't take full advantage of it.

📌 Why HSAs Are So Powerful:
✔ Contributions are tax-deductible → Reduces taxable income.
✔ Money grows tax-free → Invest in stocks, ETFs, or mutual funds.
✔ Withdrawals for medical expenses are tax-free → No penalties or taxes on qualified healthcare costs.

📌 2024 HSA Contribution Limits:
✔ $4,150 per year for individuals
✔ $8,300 per year for families
✔ $1,000 extra if you're 55+

📌 Example: Using an HSA to Build Wealth Tax-Free

- Sarah contributes $8,300 per year to her HSA.

- She invests it in S&P 500 index funds with a 10% annual return.
- After 20 years, her HSA is worth $500,000—completely tax-free.

💡 Lesson: HSAs allow you to invest tax-free while covering medical expenses—it's like a secret retirement account.

Strategy #3: Use an FSA (Flexible Spending Account) for Short-Term Medical Savings

An FSA (Flexible Spending Account) is another pre-tax savings account, but it must be used within the same year.

📌 Best Uses for an FSA:
✔ Covers co-pays, prescriptions, dental, vision, and therapy.
✔ Avoids payroll taxes, reducing taxable income.
✔ "Use-it-or-lose-it" rule → Money must be spent within the year.

📌 Example: Saving $1,200 in Taxes with an FSA

- Mike contributes $3,050 to his FSA (2024 max).
- Since FSA contributions are pre-tax, he saves $1,200 in taxes (assuming a 40% tax rate).
- He uses the FSA for dentist visits, prescriptions, and vision care—all tax-free.

💡 Lesson: Use an FSA for short-term medical expenses and an HSA for long-term, tax-free healthcare investing.

Strategy #4: Set Up a Health Reimbursement Arrangement (HRA) for Your Business

If you own a business, you can write off 100% of medical expenses through an HRA (Health Reimbursement Arrangement).

📌 How an HRA Works:
✔ Your business reimburses you for medical expenses tax-free.
✔ You deduct 100% of health costs as a business expense.
✔ Can cover insurance premiums, co-pays, prescriptions, and more.

📌 Example: Business Owner Saves $10,000 on Healthcare Costs

- Mark runs a small business and sets up an HRA.
- He pays $12,000 per year in health insurance and medical expenses.
- Instead of paying out-of-pocket, his business reimburses him tax-free.
- He deducts the $12,000 from business income, saving $4,800 in taxes (40% bracket).

💡 Lesson: HRAs allow business owners to turn healthcare into a 100% deductible business expense.

Strategy #5: Write Off Health Insurance Premiums as a Business Expense

📌 Who Can Deduct Health Insurance Premiums?
✔ Self-employed individuals (Schedule C filers).
✔ S-Corp owners (with a special payroll setup).
✔ LLCs and Corporations offering benefits to employees.

📌 Example: Saving $6,000 by Writing Off Health Insurance

- Lisa pays $15,000 per year for health insurance.
- She deducts 100% of her premiums from her taxable income.
- In the 40% tax bracket, she saves $6,000.

💡 Lesson: If you're paying for health insurance with after-tax money, you're missing a massive tax break.

How to Use Tax-Free Health Strategies in the Buy, Borrow, Die Plan

📌 Step 1: Max Out Tax-Advantaged Health Accounts → Contribute to HSAs, FSAs, or HRAs to lower taxable income.
📌 Step 2: Invest HSA Funds for Tax-Free Growth → Treat your HSA like an extra retirement account.
📌 Step 3: Use Business Deductions for Healthcare Costs → Pay for insurance premiums and medical expenses pre-tax instead of after-tax.
📌 Step 4: Pass Down Tax-Free Health Wealth → Heirs can inherit unused HSA funds tax-free for medical expenses.

📌 Example: Using an HSA to Retire with Tax-Free Medical Money

- Emma contributes $8,300 per year to her HSA for 30 years.
- With a 10% investment return, it grows to $2 million.
- She uses it for tax-free healthcare in retirement.

💡 Lesson: If you invest wisely, your HSA can pay for all your medical costs in retirement—tax-free.

43

Year-End Tax Planning

Bigger Savings in the Final Stretch

Most people wait until April 15th to think about taxes—but the wealthy start planning before the year ends to legally reduce their tax bill.

By using smart deductions, last-minute business investments, and retirement contributions, you can slash your taxable income, keep more money, and take advantage of IRS-approved loopholes before December 31st.

In this chapter, you'll learn:

◼ How to legally lower your tax bill before the year ends.
◼ Which last-minute deductions and strategies can save you thousands.
◼ How to defer income, accelerate expenses, and maximize tax-free savings.

Why Year-End Tax Planning Is Critical

📌 Most tax strategies require action before December 31st.

- If you wait until tax season, it's too late to take advantage of deductions and tax-saving opportunities.
- The wealthy use year-end tax planning to move money strategically—keeping more and paying less.

💡 Lesson: December is your last chance to legally lower your tax bill for the year.

Strategy #1: Max Out Retirement Contributions for Instant Tax Savings

One of the easiest ways to reduce taxable income is to contribute more to tax-advantaged retirement accounts.

📌 Max Contribution Limits for 2024:

Retirement Account	Max Contribution	Tax Savings
401(k) (Employee Limit)	$23,000	Tax-deductible
401(k) (Employer Match)	Up to $69,000	Tax-deductible
IRA (Traditional)	$7,000	Tax-deductible
HSA (Health Savings Account)	$4,150 (individual) / $8,300 (family)	Tax-free medical savings

📌 Example: Saving $10,000 in Taxes by Maxing Out a 401(k)

- Lisa earns $150,000 and contributes $23,000 to her 401(k).
- This lowers her taxable income to $127,000, reducing her tax bill by $7,000-$10,000, depending on her tax bracket.

💡 Lesson: Retirement contributions are the fastest way to lower taxes before year-end.

Strategy #2: Buy Business Equipment & Vehicles with Section 179

📌 Why This Works:
✔ Purchases made before December 31st are deductible THIS tax year.
✔ Applies to cars, computers, software, furniture, and heavy equipment.

📌 Top Business Purchases to Make Before Year-End:
✔ New or used business vehicle (Tesla, SUV, truck, etc.)
✔ Laptops, monitors, and office furniture
✔ Software, website upgrades, and tech subscriptions
✔ Marketing and advertising expenses

📌 Example: Buying a Business Laptop for an Instant Tax Deduction

- Mike buys a $2,500 MacBook Pro for work on December 20th.
- He deducts the full amount under Section 179.

- If he's in the 35% tax bracket, this saves him $875 in taxes.

💡 **Lesson:** If you need business equipment, buy it before December 31st to get a full write-off.

Strategy #3: Prepay Business Expenses to Reduce Taxable Income

📌 **How It Works:**

- If you have extra cash, pay next year's expenses NOW and deduct them this year.
- This works for rent, insurance, subscriptions, marketing, and training.

📌 **Examples of Prepaid Expenses That Are Deductible:**
✔ Pay rent for your office or coworking space in advance.
✔ Prepay annual subscriptions (Canva, Zoom, Adobe, etc.).
✔ Invest in marketing, courses, or coaching before year-end.

📌 **Example: Prepaying Expenses to Reduce Taxes**

- Sarah's business made $150,000 in profit.
- She prepays $10,000 in 2024 business expenses before December 31st.
- Her taxable income drops to $140,000, saving her $3,500+ in taxes.

💡 **Lesson:** If you know you'll have business expenses next year, prepaying them now can reduce your tax bill.

Strategy #4: Delay Receiving Income Until Next Year

📌 **Why It Works:**
✔ If you're close to moving into a higher tax bracket, delaying income can keep you in a lower bracket.
✔ Applies to freelancers, consultants, and business owners who invoice clients.

📌 **How to Do It:**
✔ Delay invoices until January so the income is taxed next year.
✔ Push big projects into the next tax year to lower this year's taxable income.

📌 **Example: Deferring Income to Reduce Taxes**

- John is self-employed and expects a $20,000 client payment in December.
- Instead of invoicing now, he waits until January to receive the payment.
- This keeps him in a lower tax bracket for 2024, saving him $4,000 in taxes.

💡 Lesson: Delaying income by just a few weeks can reduce your tax bracket and lower your tax bill.

Strategy #5: Make Charitable Donations for an Immediate Deduction

📌 Why It Works:
✔ Donations made before December 31st are deductible this year.
✔ Applies to cash, stocks, or even real estate donations.

📌 Best Ways to Donate for Maximum Tax Savings:
✔ Donate appreciated stocks (avoid capital gains tax).
✔ Set up a Donor-Advised Fund (DAF) to give over time.
✔ Give to 501(c)(3) charities for a full tax write-off.

📌 Example: Donating Stocks Instead of Cash

- Mark owns $10,000 worth of stock that has doubled in value.
- If he sells, he owes $1,500 in capital gains tax.
- Instead, he donates the stock to a charity, getting a $10,000 deduction and avoiding taxes.

💡 Lesson: Donating appreciated assets saves more than donating cash.

How Year-End Tax Planning Fits Into Buy, Borrow, Die

📌 Step 1: Reduce Taxable Income Before Year-End → Max out retirement, buy business equipment, prepay expenses.
📌 Step 2: Borrow Instead of Taking Taxable Income → Use a business line of credit or margin loan instead of withdrawing taxable income.
📌 Step 3: Pass Down Wealth Tax-Free → Use trusts and estate planning to transfer assets tax-efficiently.

📌 Example: How a Business Owner Uses Year-End Tax Planning to Save $25,000+

- Alex earns $300,000 from his business.

- He maxes out his 401(k) ($23,000) and HSA ($8,300).
- He buys a $75,000 SUV using Section 179.
- He prepays $15,000 in business expenses.
- His taxable income drops by $121,300, saving $30,000+ in taxes.

💡 Lesson: A few simple year-end tax moves can save you tens of thousands of dollars.

PART SEVEN

Advanced Concepts

Improving the Performance of a Buy, Borrow, Die strategy

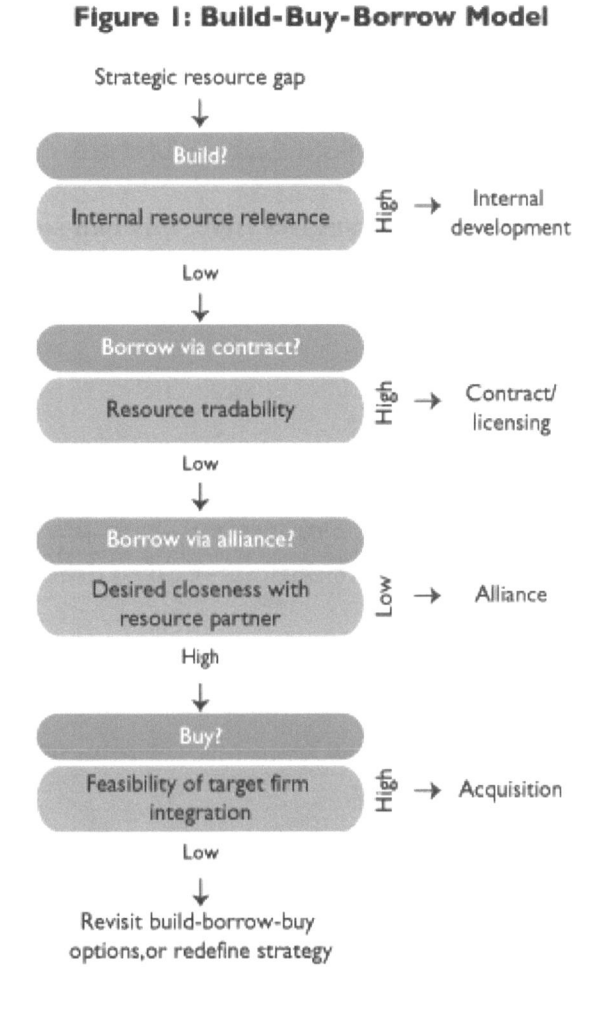

Figure 1: Build-Buy-Borrow Model

Strategic resource gap
↓
Build?
Internal resource relevance — High → Internal development
Low
↓
Borrow via contract?
Resource tradability — High → Contract/licensing
Low
↓
Borrow via alliance?
Desired closeness with resource partner — Low → Alliance
High
↓
Buy?
Feasibility of target firm integration — High → Acquisition
Low
↓
Revisit build-borrow-buy options, or redefine strategy

44

Rollover Danger

Why Great Returns May Not Be Great for You

When it comes to retirement accounts, most people focus on getting the highest returns possible. But what if I told you that a big retirement balance could actually cost you more in taxes?

That's where rollover mistakes can ruin your financial future.

The wealthy know that managing rollovers the right way can save them thousands—if not millions—in taxes. But if you do it wrong, the IRS could take a huge chunk of your hard-earned money.

In this chapter, you'll learn:

■ Why rollovers can trigger massive tax bills if done incorrectly.
■ The right way to move money between retirement accounts without penalties.
■ How to avoid Required Minimum Distributions (RMDs) draining your wealth.

What Is a Rollover and Why Does It Matter?

A rollover happens when you move money from one retirement account to another—such as from a 401(k) to an IRA.

📌 **There are two main types of rollovers:**

Type of Rollover	What Happens	Tax Consequences
Direct Rollover (Best Option)	Money moves directly from one retirement account to another (e.g., 401(k) to IRA)	No taxes or penalties
Indirect Rollover (Risky Option)	You withdraw money and deposit it into another account within 60 days	If you miss the deadline, you get hit with taxes + penalties

💡 **Lesson: Always use a direct rollover to avoid tax headaches.**

The Hidden Dangers of Indirect Rollovers

📌 Why Indirect Rollovers Are Risky:
✔ The IRS requires you to deposit the money within 60 days.
✔ If you miss the deadline, it's treated as an early withdrawal (10% penalty if under 59½).
✔ The IRS automatically withholds 20% for taxes, meaning you don't get the full balance.

📌 Example: How an Indirect Rollover Can Cost You $20,000+ in Taxes

- You withdraw $100,000 from a 401(k) and plan to roll it into an IRA.
- The IRS withholds 20% ($20,000) before you even see the money.
- If you don't come up with $20,000 from another source to complete the rollover, you owe income tax + penalties on the missing amount.
- You end up paying $30,000+ in taxes—all because of a simple mistake.

💡 Lesson: NEVER take the money yourself—always do a direct rollover.

How to Rollover Retirement Accounts Without Paying Taxes

◼ Step 1: Choose the Right Type of Rollover

✔ Direct Rollover → Best option (Avoids taxes and penalties).
✔ Indirect Rollover → Risky (Must redeposit in 60 days, or you pay taxes).

◼ Step 2: Move Money Directly Between Custodians

- Contact your 401(k) provider and request a direct rollover to an IRA (don't have them send you a check).
- If you're rolling over to a new 401(k), have the new plan administrator handle the transfer.

◼ Step 3: Make Sure the Money Lands in a Tax-Advantaged Account

- If you're rolling from a pre-tax 401(k), move it into a Traditional IRA to keep it tax-deferred.

- If you're rolling from a Roth 401(k), move it into a Roth IRA to keep withdrawals tax-free.

💡 Lesson: Using the wrong type of rollover can trigger unnecessary taxes—always move money between tax-advantaged accounts properly.

How Required Minimum Distributions (RMDs) Can Wreck Your Tax Plan

Most people forget about RMDs (Required Minimum Distributions)—but they can force you into higher tax brackets in retirement.

📌 What Are RMDs?
✔ The IRS forces you to start withdrawing money from 401(k)s and Traditional IRAs at age 73 (unless you qualify for an exception).
✔ RMDs increase taxable income, potentially pushing you into a higher tax bracket.
✔ The penalty for missing an RMD is a massive 25% of the required amount.

📌 Example: How RMDs Can Hurt You

- You retire with $2 million in a Traditional IRA.
- At age 73, the IRS forces you to take out $80,000 per year (even if you don't need the money).
- This pushes you into a higher tax bracket, increasing your Medicare premiums and reducing Social Security benefits.

💡 Lesson: RMDs can drain your retirement funds and increase taxes—unless you plan ahead.

How to Avoid RMDs and Keep More of Your Money

📌 Best Strategies to Reduce RMDs:
✔ Convert to a Roth IRA Early → Roth IRAs have NO RMDs (money grows tax-free forever).
✔ Move Money to an HSA → Health Savings Accounts have no required withdrawals and can be used for medical expenses tax-free.
✔ Donate RMDs to Charity (QCDs) → Use a Qualified Charitable Distribution (QCD) to avoid taxes on required withdrawals.

📌 Example: Using a Roth Conversion to Eliminate RMDs

- Alex has $1 million in a Traditional IRA.
- He gradually converts $50,000 per year to a Roth IRA (paying lower taxes now).
- By the time he reaches age 73, his RMDs are $0 because all his money is in a Roth IRA.

💡 Lesson: If you don't need RMDs, converting to a Roth early can save you thousands in taxes.

How Rollover Planning Fits Into the Buy, Borrow, Die Strategy

📌 Step 1: Avoid Taxable Rollovers → Use direct rollovers to prevent IRS penalties.
📌 Step 2: Move Money to Tax-Free Accounts → Convert to a Roth IRA early to eliminate RMDs.
📌 Step 3: Borrow Instead of Taking Distributions → Use tax-free loans from life insurance or real estate instead of withdrawing taxable income.
📌 Step 4: Pass Down Wealth Tax-Free → Leave heirs a Roth IRA (so they inherit money tax-free instead of paying RMDs).

📌 Example: How a High-Net-Worth Investor Avoids RMD Taxes

- Emily has $3 million in a 401(k) and is approaching RMD age (73).
- She converts $100,000 per year to a Roth IRA while in a lower tax bracket.
- She uses real estate and life insurance loans for tax-free income instead of RMDs.
- Her heirs inherit Roth IRA funds tax-free, avoiding a forced distribution tax nightmare.

💡 Lesson: If you plan ahead, you can completely avoid RMDs and pass down wealth tax-free.

45

Finding a Fiduciary

Who Wants to Play Where's Waldo?

Finding a financial advisor you can trust is like playing a game of Where's Waldo?—there are thousands of options, but only a small percentage are actually looking out for your best interests.

Most people assume all financial advisors are legally required to act in their best interest. But here's the shocking truth: many advisors work on commission, push expensive products, and prioritize their own paycheck over your financial success.

That's why you need a fiduciary—someone who is legally obligated to put your interests first.

In this chapter, you'll learn:

■ What a fiduciary is and why it matters.
■ How to spot financial advisors who are just salespeople.
■ The right questions to ask before trusting anyone with your money.

What Is a Fiduciary and Why Should You Care?

A fiduciary is a financial professional who is legally required to act in your best interest—not just sell you products that make them money.

📌 **Why You Need a Fiduciary:**
✔ **No hidden commissions** → Fiduciaries don't get kickbacks for selling you expensive investments.
✔ **Full transparency** → They must disclose any conflicts of interest.
✔ **Client-first approach** → They focus on what's best for YOU, not their employer.

📌 Example: Fiduciary vs. Non-Fiduciary Advice

Scenario	Fiduciary Advisor	Non-Fiduciary Advisor
Recommending a retirement account	Suggests a **low-cost IRA** with minimal fees	Pushes a **high-fee annuity** that pays them a commission
Investing your money	Uses **low-cost ETFs** that maximize your returns	Recommends **actively managed funds** with high fees
Disclosing fees	Clearly explains all costs	Hides fees in the fine print

💡 **Lesson:** Not all financial advisors are required to act in your best interest—only fiduciaries are.

How to Spot a Fake Fiduciary (Red Flags to Watch For)

📌 Warning Signs That an "Advisor" Is Just a Salesperson:
❌ They earn **commissions** on financial products (insurance, mutual funds, annuities).
❌ They recommend **high-fee investments** (without explaining why).
❌ They **can't clearly explain** how they get paid.
❌ They try to **rush you** into signing documents.

📌 Example: How a Fake Fiduciary Costs You Thousands

- You meet with an advisor at a major bank who recommends a high-fee mutual fund.
- The fund has a 2% annual fee, which doesn't sound like much.
- Over 30 years, that 2% fee eats up nearly **40% of your investment gains!**
- Meanwhile, the advisor earns a fat commission for selling you the fund.

💡 **Lesson:** If an advisor gets paid more when you invest in high-fee products, they have a conflict of interest.

How to Find a REAL Fiduciary (Step-by-Step Guide)

■ **Step 1: Look for These Fiduciary Credentials**

✔ **CFP® (Certified Financial Planner™)** → Has fiduciary duty & formal training.
✔ **CFA (Chartered Financial Analyst®)** → Focuses on investment management.
✔ **CPA/PFS (Certified Public Accountant – Personal Financial Specialist)** → Best for tax

planning.
- ✔ Fee-Only Financial Advisor → Only gets paid by YOU, not commissions.

💡 Avoid advisors who are "fee-based" (they may still earn commissions).

📍 Step 2: Ask These 5 Questions Before Hiring a Financial Advisor

📌 1. Are you a fiduciary 100% of the time?
✔ If they hesitate or say "sometimes," walk away.

📌 2. How do you get paid?
✔ Best answer: "I only get paid by my clients, not commissions."

📌 3. What fees do you charge?
✔ Look for flat fees or a percentage under 1% of assets.
✔ Avoid advisors who hide fees or push commission-based products.

📌 4. Will you sign a fiduciary oath in writing?
✔ A real fiduciary won't hesitate to put it in writing.

📌 5. What's your investment philosophy?
✔ Look for a long-term, low-cost strategy.
✔ Avoid anyone who pushes "hot stocks" or day trading.

💡 Lesson: The best advisors welcome transparency—if they dodge your questions, that's a red flag.

Where to Find a Fiduciary Financial Advisor

📌 Best Places to Find a Real Fiduciary Advisor:
✔ NAPFA.org → National Association of Personal Financial Advisors (Fee-Only).
✔ XY Planning Network → Great for young professionals & entrepreneurs.
✔ CFP Board's Find a Planner Tool → Certified Fiduciary Advisors.
✔ Wealthramp.com → Matches you with vetted fiduciary advisors.

📌 Avoid:
✘ Big banks & brokerage firms (Merrill Lynch, Wells Fargo, etc.) → Many of their "advisors" are really sales reps.
✘ Insurance-based advisors → Many push high-commission annuities disguised as investments.

💡 Lesson: If an advisor isn't on a fiduciary database, assume they aren't working in your best interest.

How Fiduciary Advisors Fit Into the Buy, Borrow, Die Strategy

📌 Step 1: Hire a Fiduciary to Protect Your Investments → They help you avoid high-fee products that drain your wealth.
📌 Step 2: Use Tax-Efficient Strategies → A fiduciary optimizes tax planning, Roth conversions, and estate strategies.
📌 Step 3: Borrow Against Investments Instead of Selling → Fiduciaries help you leverage assets for tax-free liquidity.
📌 Step 4: Pass Down Wealth Tax-Free → They guide you on trusts, estate planning, and minimizing estate taxes.

📌 Example: How a Fiduciary Saves You $1 Million in Hidden Fees

- Jake invests $1 million in an actively managed mutual fund (2% fee).
- Over 30 years, the fees eat up nearly $1 million in potential gains.
- A fiduciary moves him into low-cost index funds (0.05% fees).
- He saves $950,000 in fees and earns a bigger retirement nest egg.

💡 Lesson: A good fiduciary helps you grow wealth efficiently—without hidden costs.

46

Leveraging Correlation

Amplify Returns with the Buy, Borrow, Die Strategy

Most investors focus on picking the right assets, but the wealthy focus on something even more important: how their assets interact with each other.

That's where correlation comes in. Understanding correlation allows you to amplify returns, reduce risk, and build a portfolio that thrives in any economic environment.

The Buy, Borrow, Die strategy becomes even more powerful when you own assets that move differently from each other—because that's what allows you to borrow against wealth in any market condition without having to sell at a loss.

In this chapter, you'll learn:

- What correlation is and why it matters for wealth building.
- How to combine uncorrelated assets to maximize returns while reducing risk.
- How to borrow against different asset classes at the right time.

What Is Correlation and Why Should You Care?

Correlation measures how two assets move in relation to each other.

📌 **Correlation Scale:**
✔ **+1.0 (Perfect Positive Correlation):** Two assets move in the same direction.
✔ **0 (No Correlation):** Assets move independently.
✔ **-1.0 (Perfect Negative Correlation):** When one goes up, the other goes down.

💡 **Lesson:** If all your assets move together, you're not diversified—you're just exposed to the same risk in different forms.

How Correlation Affects the Buy, Borrow, Die Strategy

📌 If your assets are highly correlated:

- In a downturn, everything crashes at the same time.
- Banks get nervous and reduce loan-to-value (LTV) ratios.
- You may struggle to borrow against assets without selling at a loss.

📌 If your assets are uncorrelated:

- Some assets rise when others fall—giving you borrowing flexibility.
- You can tap into the strongest asset class at any given time.
- You never have to sell low because another asset is available to borrow against.

💡 Lesson: Owning a mix of uncorrelated assets allows you to always have a borrowing option, no matter the market.

The Best Asset Classes for an Uncorrelated Portfolio

1. Stocks (Growth & Equity Exposure)

✔ High return potential (~8-10% per year).
✔ Best for long-term wealth building.
✔ Correlates with economic growth.

📌 Best for Borrowing: Margin loans at ~5-7% interest.

💡 Lesson: Great for capital appreciation, but not ideal for borrowing in market crashes.

2. Bonds (Steady Income & Low Volatility)

✔ Less volatile than stocks.
✔ Provides stability when markets crash.
✔ Typically negatively correlated with stocks (bonds go up when stocks go down).

📌 Best for Borrowing: Secured loans at ~4-6% interest.

💡 Lesson: Bonds act as a "shock absorber" for market downturns.

3. Real Estate (Cash Flow & Asset Appreciation)

✔ Provides rental income and tax advantages.
✔ Moves independently of stocks and bonds (low correlation).
✔ Can be leveraged heavily for tax-free cash flow.

📌 Best for Borrowing: HELOCs and cash-out refinancing at ~6-8% interest.

💡 Lesson: Real estate gives you a borrowing advantage because banks love lending against physical assets.

4. Gold & Precious Metals (Inflation Hedge & Crisis Protection)

✔ Typically rises when stocks decline (negative correlation).
✔ Protects against currency devaluation and inflation.
✔ Less useful for borrowing (unless tokenized or held in ETFs).

📌 Best for Borrowing: Gold-backed loans at ~5-8% interest.

💡 Lesson: Gold is a safety net but doesn't produce cash flow—so it's better for protection than borrowing.

5. Cryptocurrency (High Risk, High Reward)

✔ Decentralized store of value (Bitcoin as "digital gold").
✔ Uncorrelated with traditional markets (but still volatile).
✔ Some platforms allow crypto-backed loans with no tax consequences.

📌 Best for Borrowing: Crypto-backed loans at ~7-12% interest.

💡 Lesson: Best used as a long-term speculative asset with borrowing potential—but riskier than other asset classes.

How to Borrow Smartly Against Different Assets

📌 The key to Buy, Borrow, Die is knowing WHEN and WHERE to borrow.

Market Condition	Best Asset to Borrow Against	Why?
Stock Market Boom	Stocks (Margin Loans)	Low rates, stocks are rising
Recession / Bear Market	Real Estate (HELOCs)	Stable, low-volatility borrowing
Inflationary Environment	Gold / Bitcoin Loans	Hard assets rise with inflation
Interest Rates Are High	Bonds / Cash Flow Assets	Protects against volatility

💡 Lesson: Smart investors borrow against their strongest asset at any given time.

How a Multi-Asset Portfolio Amplifies Buy, Borrow, Die

📌 Scenario: A Well-Diversified Wealthy Investor

- Owns: $5M in assets split across stocks, real estate, gold, and crypto.
- Stock market crashes: Instead of selling stocks, they borrow against real estate (which holds value).
- Inflation rises: They borrow against gold or Bitcoin, which are increasing in value.
- Stocks recover: They refinance their stock portfolio at lower rates.

📌 Results:
✔ Never forced to sell at a loss.
✔ Always has a tax-free borrowing option.
✔ Uses different assets to maximize liquidity and minimize risk.

💡 Lesson: A well-diversified portfolio allows you to always borrow tax-free without panic-selling assets.

47

Live off the Borrow Button

Unlocking Tax-Free Financial Freedom

Most people believe they need to sell investments to enjoy their wealth. The wealthy know better.

Instead of selling assets and triggering taxes, they borrow against their wealth tax-free—funding their lifestyle while letting their investments keep growing.

This is the secret behind the Buy, Borrow, Die strategy.

When done right, you can live tax-free, avoid capital gains, and pass down wealth without the IRS taking a cut.

In this chapter, you'll learn:

▪ How the rich borrow instead of selling to avoid taxes.
▪ The best assets to borrow against for tax-free cash flow.
▪ How to structure loans to keep borrowing without selling.

The Problem with Selling Assets

📌 What happens when you sell an investment?
✔ You trigger capital gains tax (up to 37% for short-term gains, 20% for long-term gains).
✔ You reduce your ability to compound wealth (sold assets stop growing).
✔ You lose potential tax-free borrowing power.

📌 Example: Why Selling Stocks Is a Bad Idea

- Mark owns $1M in stocks and needs $100,000 for expenses.
- If he sells $100,000, he pays 20% in capital gains tax ($20,000).
- After taxes, he only gets $80,000—losing $20,000 to the IRS.

- Worse, his investment balance shrinks to $900,000, reducing future growth.

💡 Lesson: Selling investments is expensive—borrowing against them is smarter.

How the Rich Live Tax-Free by Borrowing Instead of Selling

The wealthy never cash out their assets—instead, they borrow tax-free and let their investments keep growing.

📌 The 3-Step Borrow Button Strategy:
✔ Step 1: Buy Appreciating Assets → Stocks, real estate, ETFs, businesses, gold, Bitcoin.
✔ Step 2: Borrow Against Them Instead of Selling → Use margin loans, HELOCs, securities-backed loans.
✔ Step 3: Let Investments Keep Growing → Your assets compound, while you enjoy tax-free liquidity.

📌 Example: How Elon Musk Lives Tax-Free

- Musk owns Tesla stock but rarely sells.
- Instead, he borrows billions against his shares tax-free.
- His net worth grows, and he avoids capital gains tax.

💡 Lesson: If you never sell, you never pay capital gains tax.

The Best Assets to Borrow Against for Tax-Free Cash Flow

📌 Not all assets are great for borrowing—here's what works best:

Asset	Loan Type	Typical Loan-to-Value (LTV)	Best For
Stocks & ETFs	Margin Loans	50-70%	Fast liquidity, stock investors
Real Estate	HELOCs, Cash-Out Refinance	70-80%	Long-term tax-free cash flow
Crypto (Bitcoin, Ethereum)	Crypto Loans	30-50%	High-risk tax-free liquidity
Gold & Precious Metals	Asset-Backed Loans	50-70%	Inflation hedge
Business Ownership	Business Loans	50-80%	Entrepreneurs needing capital

💡 Lesson: The best assets to borrow against are ones that hold or increase in value over time.

How to Use Securities-Backed Loans (SBLOCs) to Live Tax-Free

📌 How SBLOCs Work:
✔ You pledge stocks, ETFs, or bonds as collateral.
✔ You borrow up to 50-70% of your portfolio's value.
✔ Interest rates are low (3-6%), and you pay no taxes on borrowed money.

📌 Example: Borrowing $500,000 from a Stock Portfolio

- Alex owns $1M in index funds.
- Instead of selling and paying $100,000 in capital gains tax,
- He borrows $500,000 tax-free at 4% interest.
- His portfolio keeps compounding, and he pays interest instead of taxes.

💡 Lesson: Borrowing against stocks allows tax-free cash flow while keeping your investments intact.

How to Use Real Estate Equity for Tax-Free Borrowing

📌 Best Real Estate Loans for Borrowing:
✔ Home Equity Line of Credit (HELOC) → Borrow up to 80% of home value, pay interest only.
✔ Cash-Out Refinance → Replace your mortgage with a new, bigger loan and take the difference tax-free.
✔ Rental Property Loans → Use rental income to cover the loan payments.

📌 Example: Using Real Estate to Access $500,000 Tax-Free

- Sarah owns a $1M rental property with $500,000 in equity.
- Instead of selling, she takes a cash-out refinance for $400,000 tax-free.
- She reinvests the money into more properties, increasing her wealth.

💡 Lesson: Real estate allows you to keep borrowing and reinvesting while avoiding capital gains tax.

How to Use Crypto Loans for Tax-Free Liquidity

📌 Why Crypto Loans Work for Borrowing:
✔ No capital gains tax → You don't sell your Bitcoin, so there's no taxable event.
✔ Instant liquidity → Many platforms offer same-day loans.
✔ No credit check → Loans are secured by your crypto holdings.

📌 Example: Borrowing $50,000 Against Bitcoin

- Jake owns 5 Bitcoin worth $250,000.
- Instead of selling and paying $50,000 in taxes,
- He borrows $100,000 at 6% interest, tax-free.
- If Bitcoin's price rises, he repays the loan and keeps the gains.

💡 Lesson: Crypto-backed loans allow tax-free liquidity but come with higher risk than traditional assets.

How to Structure Loans for Long-Term Borrowing Without Ever Selling

📌 **The Secret to Borrowing Forever Without Paying Taxes:**
✔ Borrow only what you need → Don't overleverage your portfolio.
✔ Keep debt-to-equity ratio below 50-60% → Avoid margin calls and forced sales.
✔ Refinance loans at lower rates → Use real estate and stock-backed loans.
✔ Pass down assets through estate planning → Heirs inherit tax-free with a stepped-up basis.

📌 **Example: How a Wealthy Investor Borrows for Life Without Selling**

- James owns $5M in stocks, real estate, and gold.
- Instead of selling, he borrows $500K per year to fund his lifestyle.
- His assets continue to grow, covering loan interest and appreciation.
- When he dies, his heirs inherit assets tax-free, wiping out the loan liability.

💡 **Lesson:** By borrowing instead of selling, you can maintain wealth, avoid taxes, and pass down assets tax-free.

48

Will You Own Nothing and Be Happy?

There's a controversial idea floating around—one that's been echoed by the World Economic Forum, futurists, and financial analysts alike:

"In the future, you will own nothing and be happy."

At first glance, this sounds like a dystopian nightmare—but is there some truth to it? Are we actually heading toward a world where ownership is obsolete, or are the wealthy simply evolving their strategies?

The Buy, Borrow, Die strategy proves that ownership isn't what creates wealth—control is.

In this chapter, you'll learn:

■ Why ownership is becoming less important than access.
■ How the wealthy already "own nothing" while controlling everything.
■ What this means for the future of wealth and financial freedom.

The Shift from Ownership to Access

📌 Traditionally, wealth was built through ownership:
✔ Owning land = power
✔ Owning businesses = control
✔ Owning assets = financial security

📌 But today, we're shifting toward an economy based on access:
✔ Streaming replaces DVD collections.
✔ Ride-sharing replaces car ownership.

✔ Cloud computing replaces personal servers.
✔ Subscription models replace outright purchases.

💡 Lesson: You no longer need to own everything to benefit from it.

How the Wealthy "Own Nothing" While Controlling Everything

The ultra-wealthy don't own assets in their personal names. Instead, they structure their wealth in corporations, trusts, and holding companies—legally "owning nothing" while controlling everything.

📌 The Wealthy Use These Strategies:
✔ Real estate is owned by LLCs → Protects assets from lawsuits and taxes.
✔ Businesses are held through trusts → Reduces estate taxes.
✔ Personal expenses are covered by business entities → Legally shifts tax liability.

📌 Example: How Billionaires Own Nothing (But Control Everything)

- Jeff Bezos doesn't "own" Amazon stock—his entities do.
- Elon Musk funds his lifestyle by borrowing against Tesla shares—without ever selling them.
- Wealthy families use dynasty trusts to hold assets indefinitely—avoiding estate taxes.

💡 Lesson: The rich don't focus on ownership—they focus on control and tax efficiency.

The Subscription Economy: Renting Everything Instead of Owning

📌 More industries are moving from ownership to subscription models:

Industry	Old Model (Ownership)	New Model (Subscription/Access)
Movies & Music	DVDs, CDs	Netflix, Spotify
Cars	Car ownership	Uber, Tesla subscriptions
Homes	Buying a house	Rent, Airbnb, co-living spaces
Technology	Owning software	SaaS (Software-as-a-Service)

📌 Example: Why Millennials Rent Instead of Buy

- Instead of buying homes, cars, or furniture, younger generations prefer flexibility.
- They subscribe to everything—paying for access instead of ownership.
- This frees up capital for investing, rather than tying money into depreciating assets.

💡 Lesson: The future economy will prioritize access over ownership—just like the wealthy already do.

The Dangers of Owning Nothing (If You're Not in Control)

📌 If you own nothing but have no assets or cash flow, you're financially trapped.

✔ Renting everything means you're always paying.
✔ If you don't build equity, you never escape the cycle.
✔ Governments and corporations could control access to resources.

📌 Example: The Dark Side of Owning Nothing

- If everything is rented or subscription-based, companies can increase prices at any time.
- No ownership = no assets to borrow against, keeping you reliant on income.
- Governments could limit access to financial services, property, or investments.

💡 Lesson: If you "own nothing" but also don't control assets, you could end up financially powerless.

How to "Own Nothing" Like the Wealthy (Without Being Trapped)

📌 The key isn't to own nothing—it's to control everything.

✔ Use LLCs & Trusts → Legally protect assets without personal ownership.
✔ Borrow Against Assets Instead of Selling → Keep wealth growing while accessing cash tax-free.
✔ Prioritize Income-Generating Investments → Own things that produce cash flow, not liabilities.
✔ Diversify Across Asset Classes → Stocks, real estate, crypto, and businesses for flexibility.

📌 Example: How a Smart Investor "Owns Nothing" but Controls Millions

- Sarah holds real estate in LLCs for liability protection.
- She borrows against stocks & rental income for tax-free cash flow.
- Her business expenses are paid through a corporate entity for tax benefits.
- When she passes away, her assets transfer via a trust with no estate tax.

💡 Lesson: You don't have to personally "own" things—just control them through strategic structures.

Final Thoughts: Will You Own Nothing and Be Happy?

■ Ownership is becoming less important than access.
■ The wealthy already "own nothing" by using LLCs, trusts, and borrowing strategies.
■ Renting and subscriptions offer flexibility but should not replace asset-building.
■ To stay financially free, focus on control—not just access.

💡 The Takeaway?

The phrase "You will own nothing and be happy" isn't a prediction—it's a choice.

The wealthy own nothing on paper but control assets that generate wealth. If you adopt their strategies, you can enjoy the benefits of ownership without the risks, taxes, or liabilities.

What's Next?

In the next chapter, we wrap up everything into a simple blueprint for building tax-free generational wealth using the Buy, Borrow, Die strategy.

Epilogue

The Wealth Blueprint of the Future

We've uncovered the secrets that the ultra-wealthy have been using for generations—strategies that allow them to build, protect, and pass down wealth while paying little to no taxes.

The Buy, Borrow, Die strategy isn't just a financial trick—it's a mindset shift.

Most people are trained to:
✘ Work for money.
✘ Pay taxes on every dollar earned.
✘ Save cash in the bank (losing value to inflation).
✘ Sell investments, triggering more taxes.

But the wealthy do the opposite:
■ They own appreciating assets.
■ They borrow against those assets tax-free.
■ They reinvest borrowed money to grow their wealth.
■ They pass down assets tax-free through trusts and estate planning.

The result? They keep getting richer while the average person struggles.

How You Can Start Today

You don't need to be a billionaire to use these strategies. You just need the right financial habits and the discipline to implement them.

📌 Step 1: Own the Right Assets
✔ Buy stocks, real estate, businesses, and gold—assets that increase in value.
✔ Avoid wasting money on depreciating liabilities (fancy cars, unnecessary expenses).

📌 Step 2: Borrow Instead of Selling
✔ Open a securities-backed line of credit (SBLOC) or a HELOC for liquidity.
✔ Use loans to fund expenses and reinvest in cash-flowing assets.
✔ Never sell investments just to access cash—keep assets growing.

📌 Step 3: Use Tax-Efficient Accounts
✔ Max out 401(k)s, IRAs, HSAs, and Roth accounts to shelter wealth.
✔ Deduct business expenses and reinvest tax savings.
✔ Consider a trust or LLC to protect assets long-term.

📌 Step 4: Pass Down Wealth Tax-Free
✔ Set up a family trust so your heirs inherit assets tax-free.
✔ Structure business holdings in a way that minimizes estate taxes.
✔ Teach your family how to use Buy, Borrow, Die, so wealth grows across generations.

💡 Lesson: You don't need to work forever if you build assets that work for you.

The Future of Wealth Is in Your Hands

The financial system isn't designed to make everyone rich.

Most people work hard, pay high taxes, and never escape the cycle. But if you understand how money really works, you can break free.

📌 What You've Learned in This Book:
✔ How to legally pay less tax by borrowing instead of selling.
✔ How to build a tax-free portfolio of appreciating assets.
✔ How to use the wealth-building strategies of the rich—at any income level.
✔ How to pass down wealth tax-free using trusts and estate planning.

💡 Final Lesson: The Buy, Borrow, Die strategy is the ultimate financial cheat code—if you use it wisely.

Now, it's your turn.

■ Build your assets.
■ Borrow against them tax-free.
■ Let your wealth grow for generations.

The game of money has rules. Now that you know them, play to win.

What's Next?

- Want to go deeper? → Work with a fiduciary advisor to set up your financial plan.
- Ready to build wealth? → Start applying Buy, Borrow, Die with your first investment.

- **Want to protect your legacy?** → Set up a trust and estate plan so your wealth lasts forever.

Real Estate Simplified

How to Get Wealthy with Property—The Smart Way

Real estate is one of the most powerful wealth-building tools in history. It has created more millionaires than any other asset class, and when combined with the Buy, Borrow, Die strategy, it becomes even more powerful.

But many people overcomplicate real estate investing—thinking they need to be house-flipping experts or have millions to get started.

The truth? Anyone can use real estate to build wealth—if they understand the right strategies.

In this chapter, you'll learn:

◼ Why real estate is one of the best assets to borrow against tax-free.
◼ The simplest ways to invest in property (without becoming a landlord).
◼ How to use leverage and tax breaks to grow wealth faster.

Why Real Estate Is the Ultimate Wealth-Building Asset

📌 Real estate gives you five sources of income in one investment:

✔ Appreciation → Property values tend to rise over time.
✔ Cash Flow → Rent payments provide steady income.
✔ Loan Paydown → Tenants help pay off your mortgage.
✔ Tax Benefits → Depreciation and deductions reduce taxable income.
✔ Leverage → You can buy a property with borrowed money, amplifying returns.

📌 Example: How a $50,000 Investment Turns Into $500,000+

- You buy a $500,000 rental property with $50,000 down (10%).
- Over time, the property appreciates to $1M (doubling in value).
- Your mortgage gets paid down by tenants, increasing your equity.
- You refinance tax-free, pulling out $300,000 while keeping the asset.
- Your original $50,000 investment turns into $500,000+ in wealth.

💡 Lesson: Real estate allows you to build wealth using other people's money (OPM).

The Simplest Ways to Invest in Real Estate (Without the Hassle)

You don't need to become a landlord dealing with tenants and repairs to make money in real estate. Here are three simple ways to invest without the headaches:

1. Buy Rental Properties and Use Property Management

✔ Hire a property manager (8-10% of rent) to handle tenants, repairs, and maintenance.
✔ Focus on cash-flowing properties where rent covers all expenses.
✔ Use a HELOC or cash-out refinance to buy more properties over time.

📌 Example: How to Buy a Rental with Only $20K

- You find a $200,000 rental property.
- You get a loan with 10% down ($20,000).
- Rent covers the mortgage, property manager, and expenses.
- Over time, property values rise, and you pull out equity to buy another one.

💡 Lesson: Owning rental properties doesn't have to be time-consuming—just outsource the work.

2. Invest in Real Estate Without Buying Property (REITs & Syndications)

✔ Real Estate Investment Trusts (REITs) → Own shares in large property portfolios, like stocks.
✔ Real Estate Syndications → Pool money with other investors for big real estate deals.

📌 Why This Works:
✔ No landlord responsibilities → Professionals manage everything.
✔ Liquidity → REITs can be bought and sold like stocks.
✔ Diversification → Own multiple properties with a small investment.

📌 Example: Turning $5,000 into Passive Real Estate Income

- You invest $5,000 into a real estate syndication (large apartment complex).
- Every year, you earn 8-10% in passive income.
- After 5 years, the property is sold, and you double your money.

💡 Lesson: You don't need to own physical property to profit from real estate.

3. House Hacking: Live for Free While Building Wealth

✔ Rent out extra rooms or a separate unit to cover your mortgage.
✔ Use an FHA loan (3.5% down) to buy a duplex, triplex, or fourplex.
✔ Live in one unit, rent the others—your tenants pay your mortgage.

📌 Example: How to Own a Home and Pay $0 Mortgage

- You buy a $400,000 duplex with $14,000 down (FHA loan, 3.5%).
- You live in one unit and rent the other for $2,000/month.
- Your mortgage is $2,000/month—so your tenant covers the entire payment.
- After a year, you move out and rent both units—now making $2,000/month in passive income.

💡 Lesson: House hacking is one of the easiest ways to build wealth while eliminating your housing costs.

How to Use Real Estate for Tax-Free Borrowing (Buy, Borrow, Die Strategy)

Real estate is the best asset to borrow against tax-free because banks love lending against it.

📌 How to Live Off Your Properties Tax-Free:
✔ Step 1: Buy a rental property (or multiple).
✔ Step 2: Let tenants pay down the mortgage while property values rise.
✔ Step 3: Use a cash-out refinance or HELOC to borrow money tax-free.
✔ Step 4: Reinvest borrowed money into more real estate.

📌 Example: Borrowing $500K Tax-Free from Real Estate

- Mike owns a $1M rental property with $500K in equity.
- Instead of selling, he does a cash-out refinance for $500K.
- He uses that $500K to buy another property, doubling his portfolio.
- He pays no taxes because it's a loan, not income.

💡 Lesson: Real estate lets you borrow tax-free while keeping assets growing.

Common Mistakes (And How to Avoid Them)

📌 **Mistake #1: Buying a Bad Rental Property**

- Not all real estate is a good investment.
- Solution: Only buy properties where rent covers all expenses and cash flows positive.

📌 **Mistake #2: Not Having a Cash Reserve**

- Unexpected repairs and vacancies happen.
- Solution: Keep 3-6 months of expenses in reserves for emergencies.

📌 **Mistake #3: Selling Instead of Refinancing**

- Selling triggers capital gains tax and ends your cash flow.
- Solution: Always borrow against equity instead of selling.

💡 **Lesson:** If you avoid these mistakes, real estate can create generational wealth.

How to Get Wealthy... Simplified

I remember the first time I realized wealth wasn't about how much money you made—it was about how much you kept and how you let it grow.

I was sitting across from a man who had spent his entire life earning a high salary, yet he was terrified of retirement. He had worked for decades, made good money, but had little to show for it beyond a paycheck-to-paycheck lifestyle and a retirement account that barely scratched the surface of his future expenses.

Then, I met someone else—a quiet investor who had never made more than a modest salary but had built a seven-figure net worth without stress, without luck, and without complicated financial tricks. He wasn't flashy. He wasn't a genius. He simply understood how money worked and followed a system.

The Truth About Wealth

Here's what I learned: Getting wealthy isn't about grinding endlessly or being the smartest person in the room. It's about playing the game correctly.

Wealth follows a formula—one that has worked for centuries, one that the ultra-rich follow, and one that anyone can use.

It doesn't require you to:
✘ Have a high-paying job.
✘ Start the next big company.
✘ Save every penny and live like a monk.

Instead, it requires a shift in mindset.

Step 1: Stop Trading Time for Money

Most people are stuck in a trap they don't even realize exists: they trade their time for money.

✔ Work 40+ hours → Get a paycheck.
✔ Work harder → Maybe get a raise.
✔ Stop working → No more money.

📌 The wealthy don't do this. They understand that money should work for them, not the other way around.

How to Escape the Time-for-Money Trap

- Stop focusing on earning more per hour—start focusing on building assets.
- If you have $1,000,000 invested at 8% per year, you make $80,000 annually—without working.
- Your job should be a stepping stone to buy assets, not your end goal.

💡 Lesson: If you're always trading time for money, you'll never be free.

Step 2: Buy Assets, Not Liabilities

I once met a guy who drove a brand-new Mercedes, lived in a luxury apartment, and had zero savings.

He made six figures but was broke. Why? He spent his money on liabilities—things that looked like wealth but drained his bank account.

📌 The rich don't spend on status—they spend on assets.

✔ Assets → Stocks, real estate, businesses, investments that grow in value.
✘ Liabilities → Expensive cars, designer clothes, things that lose value.

📌 Example: How Buying the Right Things Makes You Rich

- Two people each earn $100,000 per year.
- Person A buys a $50,000 car (depreciating liability).
- Person B buys $50,000 in stocks (appreciating asset).
- In 10 years, Person A's car is worth $10,000; Person B's stocks are worth $100,000+.

💡 Lesson: What you buy today determines your wealth tomorrow.

Step 3: Use Other People's Money (OPM) to Get Rich

The wealthy don't just use their own money to get richer—they use other people's money.

✔ They use bank loans to buy real estate and let tenants pay the mortgage.
✔ They use business loans to grow companies.
✔ They borrow against assets tax-free instead of selling and paying taxes.

📌 Example: How Leverage Builds Wealth Faster

- Instead of saving up $500,000 to buy a house, you use a loan and only put $50,000 down.
- The house appreciates to $1M over time.
- Your return isn't based on your $50,000 investment—it's based on the full $500,000 asset.

💡 Lesson: The wealthy know that the right kind of debt builds wealth—if it buys assets, not liabilities.

Step 4: Borrow, Don't Sell (The Wealth Cheat Code)

I once wondered why billionaires never seemed to sell anything—yet they always had money.

Then I learned the secret: They don't sell their assets. They borrow against them.

✔ If you sell stocks or real estate → You owe capital gains tax.
✔ If you borrow against them → You get cash tax-free.

📌 Example: How to Live Off Your Wealth Without Selling

- You own $2M in stocks and need cash.
- Instead of selling (and paying $400K+ in taxes), you take out a loan against your portfolio.
- You get tax-free money, and your stocks keep compounding.

💡 Lesson: Wealthy people don't cash out—they borrow and let assets grow.

Step 5: Pass Down Wealth Tax-Free

Most people build wealth the wrong way: they die, and their kids get hit with massive taxes.

The wealthy avoid this with a simple strategy:
✔ They hold assets forever.
✔ They pass them down through trusts.
✔ Their heirs inherit everything tax-free through the step-up basis rule.

📌 Example: How the Rich Pass Down Billions Tax-Free

- A billionaire dies owning $100M in real estate.
- Instead of selling, their heirs inherit at a new tax-free cost basis.
- They borrow against the properties tax-free, keeping the cycle going.

💡 Lesson: The right estate planning lets your wealth last for generations.

Your Wealth Plan (In 5 Simple Steps)

■ Step 1: Stop trading time for money—start building assets.
■ Step 2: Spend money on assets, not liabilities.
■ Step 3: Use leverage (smart debt) to grow wealth faster.
■ Step 4: Borrow against assets tax-free instead of selling.
■ Step 5: Pass down wealth through trusts and estate planning.

This is how generational wealth is built—not through luck, but through a system.

Glossary of Terms

This glossary provides clear, concise definitions of key financial concepts and strategies discussed throughout this book. Understanding these terms will help you apply the Buy, Borrow, Die strategy effectively and navigate the world of wealth-building with confidence.

A

Asset – Anything you own that has value and can generate wealth over time (e.g., stocks, real estate, businesses).

Appreciation – The increase in value of an asset over time (e.g., a property increasing from $300,000 to $500,000).

Amortization – The process of gradually paying off a loan over time through regular payments.

Annuity – A financial product that provides regular payments over time, usually for retirement.

B

Buy, Borrow, Die – A wealth-building strategy where assets are purchased, borrowed against for tax-free cash flow, and passed down tax-free to heirs.

Basis (Cost Basis) – The original value of an asset, used to calculate capital gains taxes when sold.

Brokerage Account – An investment account that allows you to buy and sell stocks, ETFs, and other securities.

Bonds – Fixed-income investments where you lend money to the government or corporations in exchange for interest payments.

Bonus Depreciation – A tax strategy that allows businesses to deduct the full cost of an asset in the first year instead of spreading it over time.

C

Capital Gains Tax – The tax you pay on profits from selling an asset like stocks or real estate.

Cash Flow – The net income from an investment after expenses (e.g., rental income minus mortgage payments).

Compound Interest – Interest earned on both the original amount and previously earned interest, allowing wealth to grow exponentially over time.

Correlation – The relationship between how two investments move in value; low or negative correlation helps diversify a portfolio.

Cryptocurrency – A digital currency that operates on blockchain technology, such as Bitcoin or Ethereum.

D

Depreciation – A tax deduction that accounts for the declining value of a property or business asset over time.

Direct Rollover – The process of moving money from one retirement account to another without triggering taxes.

Dividend – A portion of a company's profits paid to shareholders.

E

Equity – The value of an asset you own after subtracting any debt (e.g., if your home is worth $500,000 and you owe $300,000, your equity is $200,000).

ETF (Exchange-Traded Fund) – A diversified investment that tracks an index, like the S&P 500, and trades like a stock.

Estate Planning – The process of arranging how your assets will be passed down to heirs, often through trusts and wills.

F

Fiduciary – A financial advisor who is legally required to act in your best interest rather than selling high-commission products.

Foreclosure – The legal process where a lender takes ownership of a property due to missed mortgage payments.

401(k) Plan – An employer-sponsored retirement savings plan with tax benefits.

G

Gross Income – Your total earnings before taxes and deductions.

Gold-Backed Loan – A loan secured by gold or precious metals instead of cash or property.

H

HELOC (Home Equity Line of Credit) – A revolving line of credit that allows homeowners to borrow against the equity in their home.

HSA (Health Savings Account) – A tax-advantaged account that allows individuals with high-deductible health plans to save for medical expenses.

Holding Company – A company created to own assets such as real estate, stocks, or other businesses, often for tax benefits and liability protection.

I

Index Fund – A type of mutual fund or ETF that follows a market index, such as the S&P 500.

Inflation – The rise in prices over time, reducing the purchasing power of money.

IRA (Individual Retirement Account) – A tax-advantaged retirement savings account.

Interest-Only Loan – A loan where you only pay interest for a set period before paying down the principal.

L

Leverage – Using borrowed money to invest, amplifying potential returns (or losses).

Liability – Financial obligations or debts (e.g., loans, credit card balances).

LLC (Limited Liability Company) – A legal structure that protects personal assets while allowing business flexibility.

Liquidity – How easily an asset can be converted into cash without significantly affecting its value.

Loan-to-Value (LTV) Ratio – The percentage of an asset's value that a lender is willing to loan (e.g., an 80% LTV on a $500,000 home means the bank lends $400,000).

M

Margin Loan – A loan from a brokerage firm that allows investors to borrow money against their stock portfolio.

Mortgage Interest Deduction – A tax deduction for homeowners that reduces taxable income based on the amount of mortgage interest paid.

Municipal Bonds (Munis) – Tax-free bonds issued by local governments to fund projects like roads and schools.

N

Net Worth – The total value of your assets minus your liabilities.

Non-Fiduciary Advisor – A financial advisor who is not legally required to act in your best interest and may earn commissions on recommended products.

O

OPM (Other People's Money) – The concept of using borrowed funds to invest and grow wealth.

Options Trading – A financial strategy that involves contracts giving the right to buy or sell a stock at a certain price before expiration.

P

Passive Income – Income earned with minimal effort, such as rental income, dividends, or royalties.

Private Equity – Investments in private companies that are not publicly traded.

Portfolio – A collection of investments owned by an individual or entity.

Principal – The original amount of money borrowed or invested.

R

REIT (Real Estate Investment Trust) – A company that owns and operates income-producing real estate, allowing investors to earn passive income without owning property directly.

Refinancing – Replacing an existing loan with a new one, often to lower interest rates or access cash.

RMD (Required Minimum Distribution) – The minimum amount you must withdraw from retirement accounts after age 73.

Roth IRA – A retirement account where contributions are taxed upfront, but withdrawals are tax-free.

S

S-Corp – A business structure that offers tax advantages for small business owners.

SBLOC (Securities-Backed Line of Credit) – A loan that allows investors to borrow against their stock portfolio tax-free.

Step-Up in Basis – A tax rule that allows heirs to inherit assets at their current market value, eliminating capital gains taxes on past appreciation.

Stocks – Shares of ownership in a company.

T

Tax Bracket – A range of income levels taxed at a specific percentage.

Tax Loss Harvesting – A strategy to reduce capital gains taxes by selling losing investments.

Trust Fund – A legal arrangement to hold and manage assets for beneficiaries.

U

Underwriting – The process lenders use to evaluate risk before approving a loan.

Uncorrelated Assets – Investments that don't move in the same direction, reducing risk (e.g., stocks and real estate).

V

Venture Capital – Funding provided to startups and high-growth companies in exchange for equity.

Volatility – The level of fluctuation in an asset's price over time.

W

Wealth Transfer – The process of passing wealth to heirs through trusts, estates, and other tax-efficient methods.

Withholding Tax – The portion of income automatically taken out for taxes before you receive it.

Bonus Stock Report

Top Wealth-Building Stocks for Long-Term Growth

Building wealth through stocks isn't about gambling on the latest trend—it's about owning assets that grow, generate income, and allow you to borrow against them tax-free.

In this Bonus Stock Report, we'll cover:
- ■ The best long-term stocks for compounding wealth
- ■ Dividend-paying stocks that provide tax-efficient income
- ■ Low-risk ETFs for simple, hands-off investing
- ■ How to borrow against your stock portfolio instead of selling

The Ultimate Stocks for Long-Term Wealth

📌 Why These Stocks?
✔ Strong fundamentals – Companies that dominate their industries.
✔ Consistent growth – Stocks that appreciate over time.
✔ Borrowing potential – You can use these stocks as collateral for tax-free loans.

Top Long-Term Stocks for Buy, Borrow, Die

Stock (Ticker)	Why It's Great for Wealth-Building
Apple (AAPL)	Strong cash flow, dominant in tech, pays dividends
Microsoft (MSFT)	AI & cloud computing leader, consistent revenue growth
Nvidia (NVDA)	Dominates AI & GPU market, massive long-term potential
Google (GOOGL)	Digital advertising & AI giant with strong cash reserves
Amazon (AMZN)	E-commerce & cloud computing leader with global reach
Berkshire Hathaway (BRK.B)	Warren Buffett's portfolio of winning businesses
Tesla (TSLA)	EV & renewable energy innovator with global expansion

📌 Why These Stocks Matter

- They are low-risk, high-growth companies with long-term potential.
- You can borrow against them tax-free using a securities-backed loan (SBLOC).

- They let you grow wealth without selling and triggering taxes.

💡 Lesson: Wealthy investors don't trade stocks—they own the best companies for decades.

The Best Dividend Stocks for Passive Income

📌 Why Dividends Matter:
✔ Dividends provide consistent, passive income.
✔ They allow tax-efficient withdrawals while keeping stocks growing.
✔ Reinvested dividends compound wealth over time.

Top Dividend Stocks for Long-Term Investors

Stock (Ticker)	Dividend Yield (%)	Why It's a Strong Pick
Johnson & Johnson (JNJ)	2.8%	Recession-proof healthcare giant
Procter & Gamble (PG)	2.4%	Household essentials company with 60+ years of dividends
Coca-Cola (KO)	3.2%	Global brand with stable cash flow
McDonald's (MCD)	2.1%	Fast-food leader with real estate assets
PepsiCo (PEP)	2.6%	Strong brand, global distribution
ExxonMobil (XOM)	4.2%	Oil & gas giant with high dividend payouts

📌 Why These Stocks Matter

- You can live off dividend income tax-efficiently.
- These companies have decades of consistent dividend growth.
- Borrowing against dividend stocks provides both income & liquidity.

💡 Lesson: Dividends create passive income while allowing tax-free borrowing for even greater financial flexibility.

Best ETFs for Hands-Off Investing & Growth

📌 Why ETFs Are Great for Wealth-Building
✔ Diversified → Spread risk across multiple companies.
✔ Low fees → No need to worry about expensive fund managers.
✔ Long-term growth → Set it and forget it.

Top ETFs for Long-Term Investing

ETF (Ticker)	Why It's a Strong Pick
SPDR S&P 500 ETF (SPY)	Owns the top 500 U.S. companies, long-term stability
Vanguard Total Stock Market ETF (VTI)	Diversified across large-, mid-, and small-cap stocks
Vanguard Dividend Appreciation ETF (VIG)	Focuses on companies that consistently raise dividends
iShares MSCI Emerging Markets ETF (EEM)	Exposure to high-growth international markets
ARK Innovation ETF (ARKK)	High-risk, high-reward tech & disruptive innovation stocks

📌 Why These ETFs Matter

- They require no active management—set it and forget it.
- SPY and VTI allow borrowing via SBLOCs for tax-free cash flow.
- Dividend ETFs like VIG provide steady, growing income over time.

💡 Lesson: ETFs make it easy to invest long-term without picking individual stocks.

How to Borrow Against Your Stock Portfolio Tax-Free

📌 Why Selling Stocks is a Bad Idea:
✘ You trigger capital gains taxes (up to 37% on short-term sales).
✘ You lose future compounding growth on the sold stocks.
✘ You may mistime the market and sell low.

📌 How the Rich Use SBLOCs Instead
✔ They borrow against stocks (50-70% of portfolio value).
✔ They use the cash for expenses, investments, or reinvestment.
✔ They pay low interest (3-6%) while avoiding capital gains tax.

📌 Example: Borrowing $500K Tax-Free

- Alex owns $1M in SPY ETF.
- Instead of selling and paying $200K in taxes, he takes a $500K SBLOC at 4% interest.
- His stocks keep growing, and he pays only $20K per year in interest instead of $200K in taxes.

💡 Lesson: Borrowing against stocks instead of selling lets you live off your portfolio tax-free.

What's Next?

- **Ready to start investing?** → **Open a brokerage account and buy SPY or VTI to begin.**
- **Want passive income?** → **Focus on JNJ, KO, and VIG for dividends.**
- **Need tax-free liquidity?** → **Ask your broker about a securities-backed line of credit (SBLOC).**

🚀 **The time to start is now—invest in great companies, hold them, and watch your wealth multiply.**

Knowledge Quiz & Study Guide

Congratulations on making it this far! You've unlocked the wealth-building strategies that the rich have been using for generations. Now, it's time to test your understanding and make sure you can apply these principles in real life.

This Knowledge Quiz & Study Guide will:
■ Reinforce key concepts from the book.
■ Help you identify areas where you need more clarity.
■ Prepare you to start implementing the Buy, Borrow, Die strategy with confidence.

Part 1: Multiple-Choice Questions

1. What is the primary advantage of borrowing against assets instead of selling them?
A) Avoiding capital gains taxes
B) Increasing taxable income
C) Reducing asset appreciation
D) Paying higher interest rates

2. Which of the following is an example of a liability, not an asset?
A) A rental property generating positive cash flow
B) A stock portfolio earning dividends
C) A car purchased with a loan that depreciates in value
D) A business that produces passive income

3. What is an SBLOC (Securities-Backed Line of Credit)?
A) A loan secured by stocks or ETFs that allows tax-free borrowing
B) A retirement account that offers tax deductions
C) A high-interest loan used to buy cryptocurrencies
D) A government bond investment strategy

4. What is the 'step-up in basis' rule?
A) A tax rule that increases the value of inherited assets to current market value, eliminating past capital gains taxes
B) A method of increasing rental property appreciation
C) A way to avoid paying mortgage interest
D) A tax loophole only available to business owners

5. What does it mean to 'house hack'?
A) Renovating a home to increase its value
B) Buying a multi-unit property, living in one unit, and renting the others to cover mortgage costs
C) Flipping houses for quick profits
D) Investing in home automation technology

Part 2: True or False

6. Borrowing against assets results in a taxable event.
❏ True
❏ False

7. Real estate is a poor investment because it cannot generate passive income.
❏ True
❏ False

8. A dividend stock provides regular income in addition to potential price appreciation.
❏ True
❏ False

9. The Buy, Borrow, Die strategy allows you to pass down assets tax-free using trusts and estate planning.
❏ True
❏ False

10. Municipal bonds provide tax-free income, making them useful for high-income investors.
❏ True
❏ False

Part 3: Short Answer Questions

11. Explain why the wealthy prefer to borrow against their assets instead of selling them.

12. What is a good example of an appreciating asset versus a depreciating liability?

13. How can real estate investors use leverage to increase their returns?

14. Describe a situation where using a securities-backed loan (SBLOC) could provide tax-free cash flow.

15. What is one common mistake people make when it comes to wealth-building, and how can it be avoided?

Part 4: Case Studies & Application Scenarios

Scenario 1: The Borrowing Dilemma

Sarah owns $1,000,000 in a diversified stock portfolio. She needs $200,000 to fund a new business venture. She has two choices:

1. Sell $200,000 of stocks → This triggers a $40,000 capital gains tax bill, leaving her with only $160,000 after taxes.
2. Take a securities-backed loan (SBLOC) for $200,000 at a 5% interest rate → She keeps her stock portfolio intact, paying only $10,000 per year in interest.

Question: Which option is better and why?

Scenario 2: The Real Estate Investor

John is considering buying a $500,000 duplex. He has $50,000 saved and qualifies for an FHA loan with a 3.5% down payment.

His options:

1. Buy a single-family home to live in.
2. House hack the duplex—live in one unit, rent the other to cover the mortgage.

Question: What's the smarter move for long-term wealth, and why?

Scenario 3: The Retirement Planner

Michael is 45 years old and has $500,000 in a Traditional IRA. He's worried about required minimum distributions (RMDs) in retirement.

Question: What can he do now to reduce his future tax burden and ensure tax-free withdrawals?

Part 5: Action Plan—Applying What You've Learned

Your Next Steps

📌 **Step 1: Identify Your Assets**

- What appreciating assets do you currently own?
- What liabilities are draining your wealth?

📌 **Step 2: Set Up Tax-Free Borrowing Options**

- Do you have an SBLOC or HELOC available?
- Are you using real estate equity wisely?

📌 **Step 3: Maximize Passive Income & Investments**

- Are you investing in dividend stocks or rental properties?
- Are you using tax-advantaged accounts like Roth IRAs and HSAs?

📌 **Step 4: Plan for Wealth Transfer**

- Have you considered using trusts to pass down assets tax-free?
- Do you have an estate plan in place?

Final Thoughts: Your Wealth Journey Starts Now

You now have the knowledge and strategies to build, grow, and protect wealth like the ultra-rich.

🚀 The next step is action.

💡 Your challenge: Start implementing at least one strategy from this book within the next 30 days.

- Set up an SBLOC or HELOC.
- Invest in a cash-flowing asset.
- Begin estate planning for tax-free wealth transfer.

Success is simple—but only if you take action.

What's Next?

• **Want personalized guidance?** → **Find a fiduciary advisor to help you execute your wealth plan.**

• **Ready to start investing?** → **Open a brokerage account and start with ETFs or dividend stocks.**

• **Looking for passive income?** → **Research rental properties or REITs to generate steady cash flow.**

🚀 It's time to build your legacy—one smart financial move at a time.

Knowledge Quiz & Study Guide Answer Key

This answer key provides detailed explanations for all quiz questions, ensuring you fully understand the key concepts behind the Buy, Borrow, Die strategy and wealth-building principles.

Part 1: Multiple-Choice Answers

1. What is the primary advantage of borrowing against assets instead of selling them?
■ A) Avoiding capital gains taxes
📌 Explanation: When you sell an asset, you trigger capital gains taxes. Borrowing against your assets allows you to access liquidity tax-free while keeping your investments compounding.

2. Which of the following is an example of a liability, not an asset?
■ C) A car purchased with a loan that depreciates in value
📌 Explanation: A car loses value over time and doesn't generate income, making it a liability rather than an asset. Assets should appreciate or produce cash flow.

3. What is an SBLOC (Securities-Backed Line of Credit)?
■ A) A loan secured by stocks or ETFs that allows tax-free borrowing
📌 Explanation: An SBLOC lets you borrow against your stock portfolio without selling, avoiding taxes while maintaining investment growth.

4. What is the 'step-up in basis' rule?
■ A) A tax rule that increases the value of inherited assets to current market value, eliminating past capital gains taxes
📌 Explanation: When heirs inherit assets, the cost basis resets to the current market value, eliminating taxes on past appreciation—a huge tax loophole for generational wealth.

5. What does it mean to 'house hack'?
■ B) Buying a multi-unit property, living in one unit, and renting the others to cover mortgage costs
📌 Explanation: House hacking allows you to live for free or at a reduced cost by renting out part of your home while building equity.

Part 2: True or False Answers

6. Borrowing against assets results in a taxable event.
■ False
📌 Explanation: Loans are not considered taxable income, making them a key tool for tax-free liquidity.

7. Real estate is a poor investment because it cannot generate passive income.
■ False
📌 Explanation: Rental properties generate monthly cash flow while also appreciating in value, making them an excellent investment.

8. A dividend stock provides regular income in addition to potential price appreciation.
■ True
📌 Explanation: Dividend stocks pay regular cash distributions while their share price can grow over time.

9. The Buy, Borrow, Die strategy allows you to pass down assets tax-free using trusts and estate planning.
■ True
📌 Explanation: Proper estate planning allows heirs to inherit assets with a step-up in basis, avoiding capital gains taxes.

10. Municipal bonds provide tax-free income, making them useful for high-income investors.
■ True
📌 Explanation: Municipal bonds ("munis") offer tax-free interest, making them attractive to investors in high tax brackets.

Part 3: Short Answer Explanations

11. Explain why the wealthy prefer to borrow against their assets instead of selling them.
📌 Answer: Borrowing against assets allows them to access liquidity without triggering capital gains taxes, while still benefiting from appreciation and compounding returns.

12. What is a good example of an appreciating asset versus a depreciating liability?
📌 Answer: A rental property is an appreciating asset because it increases in value and generates income, while a car is a depreciating liability because it loses value over time.

13. How can real estate investors use leverage to increase their returns?

📌 Answer: Investors can use loans to buy properties with minimal money down, letting tenants pay off the mortgage, while benefiting from appreciation and cash flow.

14. Describe a situation where using a securities-backed loan (SBLOC) could provide tax-free cash flow.

📌 Answer: A retiree with a $1M stock portfolio could take out an SBLOC for $500K instead of selling stocks, avoiding capital gains taxes while still allowing investments to grow.

15. What is one common mistake people make when it comes to wealth-building, and how can it be avoided?

📌 Answer: A common mistake is trading time for money instead of investing in assets. The solution is to focus on acquiring income-generating assets like stocks, real estate, or businesses.

Part 4: Case Studies & Application Answers

Scenario 1: The Borrowing Dilemma

■ Best Option: Take the SBLOC for $200,000

📌 Explanation: Selling stocks would trigger $40,000 in capital gains taxes, leaving only $160,000 in cash. Taking an SBLOC provides $200,000 tax-free while allowing stocks to continue growing.

Scenario 2: The Real Estate Investor

■ Best Option: House hack the duplex

📌 Explanation: Living in one unit and renting the other reduces housing costs, builds equity, and creates a cash-flowing asset. A single-family home, on the other hand, is just an expense.

Scenario 3: The Retirement Planner

■ Best Strategy: Convert part of the Traditional IRA into a Roth IRA

📌 **Explanation:** By doing gradual Roth conversions now, Michael can pay lower taxes today and avoid future Required Minimum Distributions (RMDs), allowing tax-free withdrawals in retirement.

Part 5: Action Plan—Applying What You've Learned

🟦 **Your Next Steps**

📌 Step 1: Identify Your Assets

- Make a list of appreciating assets (stocks, real estate, businesses).
- Identify liabilities (cars, debt, unnecessary expenses).

📌 Step 2: Set Up Tax-Free Borrowing Options

- Check if your broker offers an SBLOC.
- If you own real estate, consider a HELOC or cash-out refinance.

📌 Step 3: Maximize Passive Income & Investments

- Buy dividend stocks (JNJ, KO, VIG) or cash-flowing rental properties.
- Invest in ETFs (SPY, VTI) for long-term growth.

📌 Step 4: Plan for Wealth Transfer

- Set up a trust to protect assets from estate taxes.
- Make sure heirs understand the step-up in basis rule to inherit wealth tax-free.

Final Thoughts: Take Action Now

🚀 Now that you've completed the quiz, the real challenge begins—taking action.

🟦 Do one of these things today:
- Open an investment account and buy an ETF or dividend stock.
- Apply for a HELOC or SBLOC for tax-free liquidity.
- Start a real estate investment plan with house hacking or rental properties.

Wealth isn't about luck—it's about playing the game strategically.

📌 The Buy, Borrow, Die strategy works best when you take action.

🚀 **Now go start building generational wealth—simplified.**

Index

This index is designed to help you quickly locate key topics, concepts, and strategies discussed throughout the book.

A

401(k) Plan – Employer-sponsored retirement savings, tax advantages, Rollover Danger (Ch. 45)

Amortization – Loan repayment over time, Real Estate (Ch. 21)

Annuity – Fixed-income investment, Tax-Savvy Health (Ch. 43)

Appreciation – Increase in asset value, Stocks & ETFs (Ch. 9), Real Estate (Ch. 21)

Asset – Anything that grows in value or generates income, Stocks & ETFs (Ch. 9), Real Estate (Ch. 21)

Augusta Rule – Tax-free rental income loophole, The Augusta Rule (Ch. 31)

B

Backdoor Roth IRA – Tax loophole for high earners, Shielding Your Wealth (Ch. 15)

Bonus Depreciation – Tax deduction for real estate investors, Bonus Depreciation (Ch. 27)

Borrow Button – Leveraging assets for tax-free cash flow, Live Off the Borrow Button (Ch. 48)

Bonds (Municipal Bonds) – Tax-free income investment, Munis for Tax-Free Money (Ch. 17)

Business Deductions – Reducing taxable income through business expenses, Tacos, Tequila, and Tax Breaks (Ch. 39)

Buy, Borrow, Die – Wealth-building strategy, Buy, Borrow, Die (Ch. 11)

C

Capital Gains Tax – Tax on profits from asset sales, Minimizing Your Tax Bill (Ch. 18)

Cash Flow – Net income from investments, Rental Properties (Ch. 21)

Cost Segregation – Boosting tax-free real estate income, Cost Segregation (Ch. 26)

Cryptocurrency – Digital currency, Bitcoin vs Bucks (Ch. 36)

Crypto Loans – Tax-free liquidity against crypto, Bitcoin ETFs (Ch. 37)

D

Depreciation – Tax deduction for asset wear and tear, Depreciation on Rental Property (Ch. 25)

Dividend Stocks – Passive income-generating stocks, SPY vs SPY vs SPY (Ch. 16)

Dynasty Trusts – Wealth transfer tool, Estate Planning (Ch. 49)

E

Estate Planning – Passing wealth tax-free, Will You Own Nothing and Be Happy? (Ch. 49)

ETFs (Exchange-Traded Funds) – Low-cost diversified stock investments, Stocks & ETFs (Ch. 9)

Equity – Ownership value in an asset, Borrowing Again (Ch. 20)

Exit Strategy – Planning for long-term financial success, Real Estate Simplified (Ch. 50)

F

Fiduciary – A financial advisor legally required to act in your best interest, Finding a Fiduciary (Ch. 46)

Financial Alchemy – Transforming bad debt into good debt, Financial Alchemy (Ch. 8)

Future-Proofing Savings – Preparing for tax law changes, Future-Proof Your Savings (Ch. 14)

G

Gold & Precious Metals – Safe-haven investments, Golden Opportunities (Ch. 38)

Gross Income – Total earnings before deductions, Year-End Tax Planning (Ch. 44)

H

HELOC (Home Equity Line of Credit) – Borrowing against home equity tax-free, Home Sweet Tax Break (Ch. 23)

House Hacking – Reducing housing costs through rental income, House Hacking (Ch. 33)

HSA (Health Savings Account) – Tax-free medical savings, Tax-Savvy Health (Ch. 43)

I

Inflation – Erosion of purchasing power, Bitcoin vs Bucks (Ch. 36)

Indexed Universal Life Insurance (IUL) – Investment & tax-avoidance tool, The Swiss

Army Knife of Investing (Ch. 35)

IRA (Traditional & Roth) – Retirement savings accounts, IRA Is a Retirement Account (Ch. 12), IRA Isn't a Retirement Account (Ch. 13)

L

Leverage – Using borrowed money to amplify wealth, Live Off the Borrow Button (Ch. 48)

Life Insurance Loans – Borrowing against policies tax-free, Maximizing the Benefits of Term Life Insurance (Ch. 34)

Liquidity – Access to cash without selling assets, Borrowing Again (Ch. 20)

LLCs for Real Estate – Protecting assets and reducing taxes, Real Estate Professional Status (Ch. 29)

Loan-to-Value (LTV) Ratio – Percentage of asset value that can be borrowed, Borrowing Again (Ch. 20)

M

Margin Loans – Borrowing against a stock portfolio, Borrowing Again (Ch. 20)

Mortgage Interest Deduction – Tax savings for homeowners, Home Sweet Tax Break (Ch. 23)

Municipal Bonds – Tax-free bond investments, Munis for Tax-Free Money (Ch. 17)

N

Net Worth – Total assets minus liabilities, Future-Proof Your Savings (Ch. 14)

Non-Fiduciary Advisor – A financial advisor who may earn commissions, Finding a Fiduciary (Ch. 46)

O

OPM (Other People's Money) – Leveraging borrowed money for investments, Leveraging OPM (Ch. 22)

Options Trading – High-risk strategy for financial markets, The Basics of Financial Alchemy (Ch. 11)

P

Passive Income – Earnings with minimal effort, Passive Income from Rental Properties (Ch. 21)

Portfolio Diversification – Spreading investments to reduce risk, Leveraging Correlation (Ch. 47)

Principal – The original amount of money borrowed or invested, Real Estate Simplified (Ch. 50)

R

Real Estate – Investment class for wealth-building, Real Estate Simplified (Ch. 50)

REIT (Real Estate Investment Trust) – Passive real estate investing, Real Estate Simplified (Ch. 50)

Rollover IRA – Moving retirement funds tax-free, Rollover Danger (Ch. 45)

Roth IRA – Tax-free retirement account, Shielding Your Wealth (Ch. 15)

S

SBLOC (Securities-Backed Line of Credit) – Borrowing against a stock portfolio, Live Off the Borrow Button (Ch. 48)

S-Corp – Business entity with tax benefits, S-Corp Secrets (Ch. 40)

Step-Up in Basis – Tax break for inherited assets, Will You Own Nothing and Be Happy? (Ch. 49)

Stocks & ETFs – Core assets for wealth-building, Stocks & ETFs (Ch. 9)

T

Tax Bracket – The percentage of income taxed at different levels, Year-End Tax Planning (Ch. 44)

Tax Loss Harvesting – Offsetting gains with losses, Turning Losses into Gains (Ch. 19)

Trust Fund – Legal structure for protecting wealth, Will You Own Nothing and Be Happy? (Ch. 49)

V

Volatility – Fluctuations in investment value, Leveraging Correlation (Ch. 47)

W

Wealth Transfer – Passing assets to heirs tax-free, Will You Own Nothing and Be Happy? (Ch. 49)

Withholding Tax – Automatic tax deductions from income, Year-End Tax Planning (Ch. 44)

ABOUT THE AUTHOR

Rory V. Brock

Rory V. Brock is a financial strategist, investor, and educator dedicated to helping individuals build generational wealth using the same strategies as the ultra-rich. With decades of experience in investment management, real estate, and tax-efficient financial planning, Rory has developed a deep understanding of how money truly works—and how everyday people can leverage the system to their advantage.

After years of working with high-net-worth individuals, Rory realized that wealth isn't just about earning more—it's about structuring finances in a way that allows assets to grow while avoiding unnecessary taxes and liabilities. His passion for financial literacy led him to develop the Buy, Borrow, Die strategy, a proven framework that allows investors to grow wealth tax-free, borrow against appreciating assets, and pass down their legacy without the IRS taking a cut.

Rory's mission is simple: to help people escape the paycheck-to-paycheck cycle, build real wealth, and achieve financial freedom. His work has been featured in finance blogs, investment podcasts, and personal wealth-building seminars, where he teaches the same financial secrets the wealthy use to stay rich for generations.

Our mission is to demystify the world of money, break down the barriers to financial freedom, and equip readers with the tools they need to build lasting wealth. Whether it's real estate, investing, tax strategies, or financial independence, our goal is to create books that help you take action.

If you found this book valuable, we'd love to hear from you! Feel free to share your success stories, questions, or feedback.

Made in United States
Troutdale, OR
04/11/2025